San Diego
WOMEN'S WEEK

Book Compliments of

SDWomensWeek.com

 NORTH **SAN DIEGO**
BUSINESS CHAMBER
CONNECTIONS START HERE.

SDBusinessChamber.com

POWERSHIFT

POWERSHIFT

Transform Any Situation, Close Any Deal,
and Achieve Any Outcome

———

DAYMOND JOHN

WITH DANIEL PAISNER

Currency
New York

Copyright © 2020 by Daymond John

Published in the United States by Currency,
an imprint of Random House, a division of
Penguin Random House LLC, New York.

CURRENCY and its colophon are trademarks of
Penguin Random House LLC.

Hardback ISBN 978-0-593-13623-2
Ebook ISBN 978-0-593-13624-9

Printed in the United States of America on acid-free paper

randomhousebooks.com

2 4 6 8 9 7 5 3 1

First Edition

Book design by Elizabeth A. D. Eno

If you always put limits on everything you do, physical or anything else, it will spread into your work and into your life. There are no limits. There are only plateaus, and you must not stay there, you must go beyond them.

—Bruce Lee

This Book Is for You

To the person who is holding this book in their hands right now and looking to make a true change in their life . . .

To the person who has a goal in mind but hasn't been able to reach it . . .

To the person who wants more for their friends and family . . .

To the person who doesn't listen to the haters who tell them their goals are crazy or unachievable . . .

To the person who doesn't wait for things to happen to them but who makes things happen . . .

To the person who feels lost . . . probably more often than they'd like to admit it . . .

This book is for *you.*

My mission is to give you the keys to take back control of your life and live from the driver's seat. You have innate and unstoppable power within you, even if you don't realize it. I know you can tap into that power.

What are you waiting for? Let's go.

CONTENTS

MY TOUGHEST NEGOTIATION EVER

The young person seated across from me is insisting that I see things her way. We're pretty far apart in our negotiations. I'm firm in my position, but so is she. In fact, she's beyond firm—she's dug in. Fully invested. Her resolve is admirable. She's like a force of nature. When she sets her mind to something, it's as good as done, and even though we appear to be at an impasse I can see her reaching into her bag of tricks for a way to close the deal. She is determined. It's almost like her life (her entire future!) is depending on how close she can come to getting exactly what she wants.

I can feel it in my bones that things are about to get tough. I tell myself to keep cool and "Shark-like," but she's hitting me on an emotional level and it's getting harder and harder to hold my ground. I can close my eyes and feel the advantage shifting to her side of the table.

I tell myself to stay strong. A part of me knows I'm being played—but I'm being played by a master. Next come the waterworks. Her tears are like kryptonite—my Achilles' heel. And yet, tears or no tears, I cannot accept a bad deal.

At last, I am pushed to make a final decision. I stumble over my words as I begin . . .

"I'm sorry, Minka," I say. "I'm not wearing the princess tiara during tea time. But what if I read you your favorite story again before bed?"

Chapter 1

THE *POWERSHIFT* PRINCIPLE

If you've ever been dragged into a negotiation with your three-year-old daughter, you probably have some idea of how that opening scene shook out. (Far as I know, there's no photographic evidence of me wearing that princess tiara, so I'll just leave it at that.)

This much is clear: Right now, in our family, Minka's got power. Even at three years old, she's figured out—mostly through trial and error and some foot stomping—that if she picks a strategy, then follows a certain sequence of steps, she can almost always get her way. It might take a tantrum, followed by a sweet, knowing smile. Or it might call for a perfectly timed hug when I'm least expecting it. Either way, she'll eventually wear me down.

And she *knows* it. She knows she can get what she wants from me—and I guess it follows that one of the reasons I'm so quick to cave when she pours it on thick like this is because I know it, too. We've fallen into a kind of default pattern where Minka's strengths as a negotiator bump up against my weaknesses as a big old softie.

Keep in mind, it's not just me, jumping to Minka's whims. She's got a different approach for her mother, for her nanny, for everyone in her little life. She reads the room and changes her game depending on the players, depending on the situation.

Minka's figured out what works all on her own—because, just saying, there's no Mommy & Me class on negotiation strategies, no playgroup to help her learn to push her daddy's buttons. However, there is the benefit of experience, and here my little girl is smart enough to know that if a certain type of behavior gets results on Day One there's a good chance it'll work again on Day Next.

There's only one way I know of to transform this dynamic: through a concept I call *powershift*.

Let me tell you about the *powershift* and how I've come to embrace the concept behind it.

In my previous books, I've written about a couple principles that have powered me in my career. Early on, back when I was starting FUBU out of my mother's house in

Hollis, Queens, it was all about making things happen without any money. That's the "power of broke"—a power I tapped at an early age, and I still reach for it today.

Then, once I was coming up in the world of fashion and starting to see some success, I was all about the hustle: working hard, pushing through, and sticking to a game plan. Back then it was: How early do you get at it each day, and how late do you keep at it . . . and, even more important, how do you fill the time in between? That's the power of "rise and grind," the take-charge mindset that drives our days.

But one of the things I'm realizing lately is that **none of the blessings or successes that have come my way would have happened without the ability to shift power—from other people to myself, from myself to other people, from one area of strength to another whole new area of strength.** Those shifts powered the trajectory of my life and career, but I haven't written about them in my previous books because I didn't identify them for what they were until recently. But you better believe they're a big part of how I got where I am today. And now I want to share them with you.

Whenever I sit down to write a new book, I pay attention to what I'm hearing from my readers, who reach out to me on social media or connect with me after one of my speeches or through my online courses. With *Rise and Grind,* for example, people wanted to know how I structure my days and where I look for motivation, so I spent some time looking at ways truly successful people organize their time and kick their ambition into drive. Here, I kept hearing from people who wanted some guidance on how to build the kind of foundation they need to achieve, sustain, and grow their power base, so I've spent some time looking at the ways I've managed to do these things in my own life and career. Like I said, some of this stuff came naturally to me, in the beginning, but as I moved on I started looking at ways to replicate that success as I pivoted into other areas, away from FUBU and fashion. This book is the result of all that. It's my take on what it takes to find the power in the room, in any situation, and to put it to use in a meaningful and lasting way.

So here at the very beginning of our journey in these pages, let me put it to you plain: What is stopping you from achieving the success you desire, the success you believe you deserve? It's a simple question, really, and you don't need me to be the one asking it. You should be asking it of yourself. Maybe you already are. Maybe that's why you've picked up this book. Don't know about you, but I look at all the people I've known in my life, all the people I've left behind in the 'hood, all the people I've met who are still struggling to find a purposeful path, and I can't understand why they're still making excuses for being stuck or disappointed or over-looked for this or that opportunity. Obviously, they're not all making excuses, but trust me, I hear a lot of woe-is-me type stories. And when I do, I can't help but think, *Hey, if my dumb ass can make it, anybody can,* so here I want to shine a light on how to find that extra gear and put everything into play in a way that allows readers to tap their *powershift* potential.

This ability to turn every situation to some kind of advantage is hardwired in all of us. The key is learning how to *recognize and tap into* that power that you already have within you. This book will deconstruct this process for you and show you exactly how to do it.

Me, I was a little late figuring it all out. Doesn't mean I wasn't using that power. I was using it all right, but it was a hit-or-miss type deal. As a kid, I was always able to get what I needed from my teachers, my friends in the neighborhood, and the other kids at school . . . from my bosses, even, once I started punching the clock. (My mother was a whole other story—she never let me get away with anything, was always on my case, but out of all that she taught me how to work all these other relationships to some kind of advantage.) I wasn't being calculating or manipulative; I was just doing my thing. For whatever reason, I had this knack for making things happen, and it almost always happened for me in a seat-of-the-pants way. It was organic, instinctive: I never went to business school. I never went to college. Even high school was difficult for me. I came from a tough neighborhood. I struggled with dyslexia. And I wanted to learn about things beyond the basic subjects taught in school; things that were happening in the real world, outside the four walls of the classroom. The School of Life was where I learned how to get the edge I'm talking about. For that, I was able to tap something that was already in me, and I've come to believe this same something lies in each one of us.

Bottom line: I had power . . . and you have it, too. It's innate to our species, this ability we all share to put ourselves in a position to succeed—a basic survival instinct that's built into our personalities. Trou-

**ble is, most of us don't recognize this ability to
transform our own outcomes for what it is, or figure out how to use it in ways that move us forward.**

Eventually, I figured it out. But then, as I moved on in my
career, taking on newer and bigger challenges, I wanted to
understand it, perhaps even replicate it. So I looked back at
the choices I made, the approaches I took, hoping to maybe
learn something from the making-it-up-as-I-go-along ways
I've gotten to where I am today—not just to help myself
with whatever came next, but to help other people as well.
So what I hope to do in the pages ahead is break the *powershift* idea down in such a way that you'll come away from
this book even better positioned to take on your next challenge and make changes in your life, immediately.

OKAY, THEN—SO WHAT IS A *POWERSHIFT*?
POWERSHIFT /pou(ə)r • shift/

> 1. Taking control and creating moments of true change
> that allow you to live a happier, more fulfilled life
> 2. Tapping into your ability to build influence, to nego-
> tiate for the things you need and want, and to nurture
> your relationships to take you where you want to go

Let's face it, far too many people simply take what
they're given, even though we're wired in ways that can
bring us so much more. We allow ourselves to be carried by
whatever wave or moving sidewalk we happen to be on,

and it's easy to feel like we're just along for the ride. But here's the thing: There's an extra gear to our motors that most people never even find. It doesn't matter if you're looking to partner with an investor to grow your business, angling to leverage your experience and network for a big promotion, pulling out all the stops trying to convince your kid to go to bed . . . the fundamentals are all the same. The ingredients are all there. We just need to recognize them and put them to work for us.

If you've read my very first book, *Display of Power,* you might remember a story I told about a trip I took to Vegas, early on in my FUBU days. I was in a cab on my way to the convention center. We pulled up at a light and happened to slide in next to two antique Chevy sports coupes—different colors but the exact same model. Those cars were hot. It worked out that each car was at the head of its lane, waiting for the light to turn—looked like it could have been the setup for a drag race, until you looked a little more closely at who was behind the wheels. One car was being driven by a sweet older lady. (What she was doing driving such a sweet sports car, I couldn't tell you.) Behind the wheel of the other car was this youngish guy, about the same age as me. When the light finally turned, the old lady eased herself along and continued slowly on her way, while the young guy stomped on the gas and burned some serious rubber. I think he even fishtailed a little as he tore off—you know, for dramatic effect.

The cabbie turned to me and said, "Dude's gonna get a display-of-power ticket."

I'd never heard the term before, and it struck me as something I needed to understand, so I asked him to explain.

He said, "Same two cars. That lady's got no idea the kind of power she's sitting on. And that young fella, he's sitting on so much power he wants to show it to you all at once. He's got so much adrenaline, you've got to hold him back."

I've thought about that moment a lot over the years. It made an impression. That old lady, I bet the thought never even popped into her mind that she should gun her engine and strut her stuff in that car. She was just happy to be rollin' in a classic set of wheels—probably had it since the year it came out. That car had an engine with some serious horsepower—but that power meant something completely different to her than it did to the guy the next lane over. To him, it was all about the speed, the muscle; and it left me thinking he was the kind of person who attacked life in a balls-to-the-wall kind of way, all-in, all the time. So you had a situation where the same car—the same power— served a completely different purpose for these two completely different people. That difference was in how they chose to use it—or not.

When I shared that story in my first book, it meant something completely different to me. Back then, I saw it as a metaphor for the way two people can be given the exact same set of tools, but only one of them can figure out how to use them to full advantage. Now I see it from a whole new perspective. Now I see that the power of that vehicle meant different things to these two people. To the older woman, she maybe drew confidence from the style of the car, the solid frame, the don't-mess-with-me image she put out into the world when she was driving it. To the young guy, he was maybe drawn to the speed of the engine, the raw power under his hood.

What's the greatest thing about driving a sports car like one of those great muscle cars? For me, it's the way we're able to drop into a lower gear and tap the full power of the engine, the way we get going at full speed and shift into a higher gear to maybe save a little gas. Don't know about you, but I just love that moment when I'm driving and I get a chance to shift on the fly like that. It feels to me like I'm in complete control of my environment. Like anything can happen. It's all right there at my fingertips.

If you ask me, there are two kinds of people in this world. There are people like that old lady, who have the power to gun that engine but don't. And there are people like that young guy, who live life with their foot on the gas pedal, gunning that engine for all that it's worth. I'm not here to say any one approach is better than another. There's power in each line of attack—it's just a matter of how you look at it, and how you mean to draw on it.

The *powershift* I'm asking you to consider in these pages applies to those pivotal, do-or-die type moments that find us when we need to step on the gas, those moments when we have the opportunity to shoot past everyone else's expectations, or to turn on a dime and accelerate in an entirely new direction. That's what I call a *powershift,* and in the pages ahead, I'll show you how to put it to work.

THE ROAD I'M ON

Looking back, I've had to *powershift* many times in my life, starting when I was twelve years old and my father was no longer around. Even though I was just a kid, I had to learn how to be the man of the house.

Then I had to shift again when I was eighteen, growing up in a tough neighborhood like Hollis, where it had been taught to me and my boys that we would all be dead or in jail by the time we were twenty-one. I didn't like either one of those options, so after high school I told myself I'd take a year off before going to college and took a job serving shrimp at Red Lobster. I didn't have a plan. I didn't have a goal. I just needed to hustle, and here it kind of sucked that I had to serve my friends shrimp, but hustle is hustle—I needed a job, plain and simple.

When I decided to work full-time at Red Lobster, that was a real moment of clarity for me. A chance to reset. I'd realized that even though I was always moving, constantly chasing a buck, I wasn't really getting ahead. To sum it up, I felt like a failure. I wasn't living to work—I was working to live. There's a difference. So I took the opportunity to put my hustle on pause and punch the clock at Red Lobster, maybe buy myself some time to figure out my next move.

Jump ahead another few years, when we were getting FUBU off the ground, and my whole life was leveraged to the max. If things didn't break my way—and soon!—I would have lost our house, which I'd turned into our factory and warehouse. But because I was sincere in my belief that the clothes we were making would be a kind of pathway to community, I was able to shift into a whole other gear. I redirected my focus, and my power, from one type of hustle to another, and made the initial deal with Bruce and Norman Weisfeld, of Samsung's textile division, that got things started for us in a meaningful way. These guys would become my good friends and great partners, but they didn't know what to make of me at our first meeting. I guess I can't really blame them, considering that I brought my mother with me. The thing was, I'd been turned down by every bank in town when we were out looking for financing, so for this one opportunity I thought maybe I could shift the situation to my advantage by doing things a bit differently. Sure, I'd catch a lot of grief for this over the years, for being the guy who brought his mama along to do a deal, but she had my back. In fact, it was my mother who took out the classified ad in *The New York Times* that got us in that room in the first place—even though I told her it seemed like a dumb idea to look for business help with an ad. She didn't even tell me when she did it—she just placed a couple lines directed at fashion industry investors, saying we had like a million dollars in orders we needed help fulfilling. That one ad got us a ton of calls, and a couple of legit meetings . . . so hell yeah, I took my mother along for the ride—not just because she's my mother but because she's so smart.

You know, it's interesting. People wouldn't have thought twice if I'd brought my attorney with me to that meeting.

Nobody would have blinked if I'd brought a financial adviser or a mentor from the fashion industry. But because it was my mother, it raised a couple of eyebrows. Why is that? I mean, my mother was brilliant—in all kinds of ways—but her business instincts were sharp. Why can't somebody be your mother and be brilliant at the same time?

It's a great lesson: When you're looking to shift power to your side of the table, it helps to bring some extra weight along to tip the scales your way. Back then, my mother was my comfort zone. My strength. She was whip-smart (still is!), could spot a line of bullshit from a mile away (still can!), so as we rode to that meeting on one of the upper floors of the Empire State Building she gave me the confidence to believe, *We got this.*

And it turned out, we did.

By the time I was thirty-one, thirty-two, I needed to *powershift* again. For a while, FUBU was on top of the world—man, we were on *fire!* But then, a couple years in, things started to cool down a little bit. On the surface we looked like we were still going strong, but when you pulled back the curtain you could see we were starting to take a nosedive. I'm not proud of it, but the fact is, I was a little out of control in those years. I was running around, being irresponsible from time to time. In retrospect, I think I had it in my head that I was just this street kid who'd somehow won the lottery with this one fashion brand concept. I was out there working double-time, extra-hard, super-determined to make sure I wasn't some kind of one-hit wonder. Yeah, we'd caught lightning in a bottle with FUBU, but I was determined to catch some lightning a second time . . . and a third . . . and on and on. In the middle of all that craziness and uncertainty, I lost my family (more on that later), so you better believe it was a challenging time.

Eventually, I decided I was done spiraling and was able to set things right. I took my power back—from my own recklessness, and from the bad habits that had taken hold—and began putting out a whole new energy that helped me discover exciting new opportunities to invest in and buy companies and explore exciting ventures away from our FUBU core.

Then at forty, I shifted again, into a whole new gear. That's around the time *Shark Tank* happened, and suddenly I was pivoting from the familiar world of fashion into the very *un*familiar world of television. While before I was what I consider a "notable person" with my FUBU success, now I definitely was seen by ten million households on a weekly basis. But TV was a major culture shock, no doubt about it. But pretty soon, business at my consulting firm The Shark Group was popping. I had endorsement deals with major brands that I admired. *Shark Tank* was in its eighth season and firing on all cylinders. And—trust me, no one was more surprised by this than me—I'd become the author of several *New York Times* bestselling books.

But turning fifty this past year, that worked out to be the biggest shift of all—the one that lifted me onto a more purposeful path. There's a story to how that came about, and it goes like this: I'd started taking better care of myself in recent years, after talking to so many CEOs and executives who (like me!) worried constantly about their health and the continued well-being of their employees. My friend and mentor Bernie Yuman, the manager of Siegfried & Roy and overall connector in the Las Vegas scene, suggested I undergo something called an "executive physical"—basically, a turbo-charged, comprehensive battery of tests, not usually covered by insurance, taken over a couple days at some top-tier medical facility. He put the idea in my head at a time in my life when I had a whole lot going on. I had forty, fifty people on the payroll, and thousands of other hardworking souls working for my investment partners from *Shark Tank* and outside investors who were counting on me to do right by my commitment to them. I had my older daughters, Destiny and Yasmeen, leaning into young adulthood and counting on their old man for guidance and support. And at home, I had my wife, Heather, and our precious toddler, Minka, to look after, along with my mother living on her own . . . so yeah, I had everything to live for, every reason to take good care of myself.

So I followed Bernie's lead and signed up for one of these executive physicals—and it's a good thing, too, because one of the tests revealed a small growth on my neck that turned out to be stage II thyroid cancer. Oh, man . . . when the pathology came back on that sucker, it just about floored me.

Cancer.

That's a serious wake-up call. Scared the plain crap out of me. Really, there's no way to overstate it. But the good news is that the doctors caught it and removed it and at the time they said it looked like they'd got all of it—that is, until a year or so later when it was looking like maybe they hadn't. You see, one of the things you face with this type of cancer is a lifetime of follow-ups. That was my new reality. You tell yourself you can breathe easy, but in reality you're always waiting for some other shoe to drop. Every six months, I'd go in to get checked to make sure the cancer hadn't spread or come back, and on this one visit the doctor said there was a bump on my lymph nodes. Now, a bump on my lymph nodes could mean a bunch of things. It could just be the way my body was responding to the trauma of the surgery I'd had the year before, or it could mean that the cancer had spread—not the most encouraging diagnosis, but not conclusive, either. I mean, it could have been nothing, and it could have been everything.

After they did the biopsy, they told me it would take about a week for the results to come back—and let me tell you, that week felt like a year. I remembered the agonizing wait the last time around, when they took out that first nodule and I had to wait three or four days before I learned I had stage II cancer—so, you know, I had some history with this type of thing.

I spent most of those ten or so days alone with my thoughts. Mostly, I was negotiating with myself, looking at all these different outcomes. Everything was on the table— life and death and everything in between. It's not like me to think about worst-case scenarios, but when they tell you there's a chance the cancer could have spread to your brain, you tend to lose a little of your resolve, so **I pushed myself to take a hard look at the life I'd lived to this**

point. **It was like a dozen lives, really. I'd been everywhere, met just about everyone. I'd made a bunch
of money, accomplished *way* more than I'd ever
dreamed.** And the best part was that I hadn't done it just
for myself. I'd been able to provide work for thousands of
people—not just work but a salary and benefits—an exciting career. I'd shown the world that four young black men
from Queens could create a multibillion-dollar brand, I'd
had the honor of traveling the world with President Obama
to promote entrepreneurship, and I'd had the opportunity
to share my insights and experiences with millions of aspiring entrepreneurs through my books and education programs and keynote lecture appearances and television. Not
bad for a dyslexic kid who grew up thinking he'd never
make it past twenty-one. So to be looking down the barrel
at fifty, with all these great things in the rearview . . . in so
many ways, it was gratifying.

If this was God's way of telling me my time was up, I
told myself I could be at peace with that. My older girls
would be okay. My little girl was blessed with a terrific
mother, and even though every little girl needs her daddy I
knew they'd be okay. My mother . . . nobody should ever
have to bury their child, but she is a strong, proud woman,
and I knew she'd be okay, too.

During that long week, me waiting to find out if my
cancer had spread, me trying to make peace with whatever
I was or wasn't about to hear back from the doctor, I finally
decided to do something about this dark mood I was in.
The negotiations I was having with myself started leaning

to the good, and I decided it was time for a total mind–body reset. I started doing acupuncture, eating healthy, working out again—all while I was still waiting to hear back on the pathology. It was like a complete one-eighty.

What other choice did I have, really? I mean, it's not like I was going to throw up my hands and say "Screw it." After powering through that dark funk of not knowing what was going on with me, after not knowing if I was truly sick or just a little worn out, I guess I could have stopped working, started telling everyone what I *really* thought of them; I could've started drinking as much as possible, going on as many vacations as I could, living life to the fullest because I didn't know how long I had on this rock. But instead, I forced myself to take inventory.

It's like I put the cancer out of my mind—the idea of cancer, anyway. I told myself that even if the results came back against me, I wouldn't let it stop me. I would still be out there going at life full-throttle. I'd just refuse to accept a bad diagnosis, and keep living my life and working my angles and taking care of all of the people who were depending on me. I didn't know any different, wouldn't accept any different.

This, too, was a *powershift,* I started to realize, even though it had nothing to do with my businesses or my career. This was me grabbing at what was good and true, at what was possible, and applying the relentless mindset that had taken me to all the great successes I'd had to date. **It was me making a conscious decision to take control, and putting myself back in a position where I could continue to get the most out of each and**

every day. And do you want to know something? By the time I *did* finally get the pathology back at the end of that next week, I'd almost forgotten I was waiting on that call from the doctor, because nothing was going to stop me.

In my mind, I'd found a way to take the power back from the cancer that may or may not have returned and shift it back to me.

PUTTING IT ALL TOGETHER

Not long ago, I was doing a speaking gig when this guy came up to me afterward and asked for advice. He told me he was a big *Shark Tank* fan, said he watched it with his kids all the time. His kids needed a little help talking to their mother, he said. She was always shooting them down, whenever they went to her about something, and he thought maybe I could help.

The ask seemed a little out there for *Shark Tank*. Usually, I'll get bombarded with questions about guerrilla marketing strategies, or distribution issues, or warehousing and shipping issues—you know, basic entrepreneurial headaches. But here this guy was telling me his kids were having a hard time negotiating with their mother over things like schoolwork, extracurricular activities, curfews, and allowances. I didn't know what to say to this guy—not right away. But then I reached for this little lesson I'd been working on to help communicate this *powershift* concept. I thought it might be helpful, so I went right into it.

I said, "You know who Genghis Khan is, right?"

The guy nodded, but at the same time I noticed he was looking at me kind of funny—like he couldn't think where I was going with this.

I said, "He was one of history's great conquerors, right?"

Again, the guy nodded, and I proceeded to walk him through a long, convoluted story about how ten years before Genghis Khan would wage a battle, he'd start doing his homework—because, really, the preparation that went into some of these conflicts was just epic. He played the long game. He'd dispatch his armies into a region and have them move these giant boulders to divert the flow of a river, say, because he was laying in that foundation I talk about, setting himself up to succeed. The people had no idea what he was doing, but ten years later everyone looked up and he'd given himself this great advantage, because the people who had been tending that land for the past two hundred years no longer had any idea how to protect it. Khan's armies had created a whole new battlefield, before the battle had even begun. It was almost like he was playing chess, while all around him everyone else was playing checkers.

This poor guy had no idea what I was talking about, but I still had his attention, so I finally said, "Your kids, they need to create a new battlefield. They need to spend some time laying a foundation before they even talk to their mother about whatever's going on. They need to clean up their rooms, do their homework, take out the garbage, whatever they're supposed to be doing around the house."

Essentially, I was telling this guy that if his kids wanted to influence their mother's decisions, they needed to lay the foundation. They needed to build up their reputations and generate a certain amount of goodwill before reaching out to their mother for whatever it is they wanted. They needed to think two, four, ten steps ahead. And even then, once they were good and ready, they needed to present what they were asking for as a win for *both* sides, because that's how you need to negotiate, even when you're coming at it from a place of strength. You need to give as much as you get, and if it works out that you don't quite get what you want out of the deal . . . well, you've got to be gracious in defeat. Whether the person on the other side of the table is a client or customer, a business partner, an investor, or a family member, you've got to thank them for their consideration and leave the door open in such a way that you can reach back out and try for it again—you have to keep nurturing the relationship, even after you've been disappointed, because the first *no* you hear from someone won't necessarily be the final answer.

After I'd laid it all out for this guy, he seemed to get it.

I said, "That's what you call a *powershift*. You tell your kids to set it up so they have every chance to succeed, and even if they fall short, they should stay in the game—doing more chores, more homework, more of whatever it's gonna take to bring that power back to their side of the table."

True and lasting success is all about taking it to the next level, but in order to get there we first have to stand on a strong foundation. The book you're about to read will focus on the three core elements—influence, negotiation, and relationships—you'll need to put in place if you want to position yourself to take good and full advantage of the *powershift* opportunities that will find you along the way. Think of it like a three-legged stool; you'll need all three to work in sync if you mean to get and keep ahead, and you'll need to call on them all if you want them to work for you in a meaningful way. Ignore any one of them, and your entire enterprise will topple right over.

So in Part I of the book, we'll talk about the importance of building the kind of **influence** you'll need to get people to take you seriously, establish a successful track record, and do the hard work of proving your credibility and developing a reputation. In other words, you'll learn how to **make an impression.** Remember, your word is your bond—in the boardroom, in the bedroom, and anywhere else—so this is where you learn to let your reputation speak for itself.

These days, the word *influence* has taken on a whole new meaning thanks to the power of social media. In many ways, we are living in the age of the influencer—but true influence isn't about how many likes you get or how many followers you have. Whether it's online or offline, it's about developing a brand or a reputation or a persona that reflects who you are and what you stand for.

In Part II, we'll take a look at what it takes to **make a deal** from a position of strength—in other words, the negotiating skills to get what you want. While some people get clouded (and in some ways overthink them too much), I can assure you that if my little Minka can get a grasp on them, you'll see they aren't difficult to understand, either. Now, I get it that there are tons of books about negotiation out there.

Just to be clear, I'm not here to offer the same old tips and strategies you can get anywhere. And I'm not here to play the professor. Honestly, advocating for what you want is a relatively intuitive action. And I'm definitely not here to give you some complex model or hard-to-digest process. I know I personally like to learn in simpler terms, and here I'm hoping to share some straightforward insights on how you can build on top of the influence you worked so hard to establish, and create a kind of competitive edge that will allow you to seize any deal-making opportunity that presents itself.

The way we do this, at work and at home, is by learning to read the room more effectively, and by getting better at understanding what it is we hope to get from each and every transaction—that's the essence of negotiating, really. Got to say, my negotiating style as a successful entrepreneur with years of experience and a proven track record is completely different from what it was when I was a hungry, hustling kid from the streets of Hollis, Queens, just trying to get and keep ahead. But even though I'm coming at each transaction from a different place these days, I'm still the same person underneath each negotiation, so my style is true to the person I was back then—the only difference to my game, really, is that I'm using what I've learned and standing on what I've built in order to ratchet things up to the next level.

Finally, in Part III, we'll spend some time looking at why and how you need to **make relationships last**—specifically, how to establish a shared history that allows you to call on the same people again and again. If there's one thing I've learned in my career, it's the importance of nurturing relationships with people. Especially people that I've already done a deal with. Basically, you've got to establish goodwill in your partnerships with clients, colleagues, and customers, as well as with friends and family and romantic partners. And then you've got to learn to tap the goodwill you've baked into those relationships without *drawing it down* to where you've got nothing left. This is where you need to have that realization that we're in this thing not just for the moment but for the long haul. When you've driven the hell out of a relationship with someone, when you've helped each other out consistently with advice or support or money or whatever it is, you've set it up so that this person will always be in your corner, the same way you'll always be in theirs.

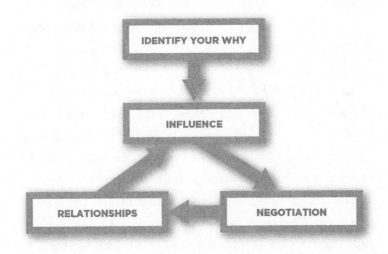

Let's take a look at those three foundational elements again:

1. Influence

Write your story, tell it to the world, work on your credibility, build a foundation of achievement, integrity, commitment, and put it out there that you mean business.

2. Negotiation

Develop a negotiating style that allows you to make the most of existing opportunities, and to create new ones.

3. Relationships

Set it up so that the people you've worked with in the past will want to work with you again in the future. Build a network of friends and contacts who are always looking to support one another and push one another forward.

Getting these three pieces working together is what the *powershift* is all about, and I hope you'll follow along with me and find some takeaways to help you navigate your own life and career with more confidence, with more certainty, and with more direction.

Here's the good news: I also created special video content and a workbook to make sure you're staying on track and creating your own *powershift*. This exclusive content is just for people who bought this book, and it can be accessed at DaymondJohn.com/PowershiftExtras.

Chapter 2

MOTIVATION FOR LIGHT

If I were to ask you the number one reason people don't get close to achieving their hopes and dreams, what would your answer be?

Would you tell me it's because they've started from a place of disadvantage?

Would you say it has something to do with unrealistic expectations?

Would you point to a bad boss, a bad economy, or some other barrier to achievement, opportunity, or reward?

We've all got our excuses to explain away a failure or disappointment, and these are damn good ones. Some of them, I wouldn't even call excuses—they're more like reasonable explanations. You can always find a million reasons why something didn't happen, but it's up to you to find the one reason why it did happen. And that one reason better be a good reason. But the *biggest* reason most people fall short of their goals, outside of health challenges, is simply that they don't take the time to think them through. They put it out there that they want to make partner, or they want to make a million dollars, or they want to start this or that business, but they don't stop to think about *why* they want these things, or *how* these things might actually impact their lives. They just hop on the moving sidewalk of life and let it take them where everyone else is going.

Back in the day, when I was hanging 'round all those video sets trying to get all those rappers and hip-hop artists to wear our clothes in their videos, I decided to take a filmmaking course at the New York Film Academy. I wanted to know what the hell I was talking about, what everyone else was talking about. This was me, doing my homework, laying in a foundation, going the extra mile . . . all of that. It had nothing to do with designing a clothing line, but in my mind it had everything to do with shifting the power in my favor, so I went out and learned what I could. One of the things I learned was a term called *motivation for light,* which I'm pinching here for the title of this chapter. Why? Well, to a lighting director, that's the single most important factor when you're setting up a shot. Doesn't matter if it's random light, a filter light, sunlight . . . whatever. If there's a light in a shot, on a character's face, you damn well better know why it's there. They've even got an acronym for it: MFL. Once you learn about it, you'll never watch a movie the same way. You'll see a scene lit by candlelight, or a sliver of light creeping in through the crack of a closed door, or through a half-opened shade on a window, and you'll know it's been discussed and considered into the ground.

So I ask you, what's your motivation for light? What are you looking to highlight or illuminate in your life or career? In other words, what is your why?

I'm reminded here of that great line from *Friday Night Lights*—"Clear eyes, full hearts, can't lose." Clear eyes, to me, means having a plan, a clear set of goals, maybe even a specific outcome. Get that covered, and you're that much closer to getting it done. How much closer? Well, according to a 2017 project management study put out by PMI Pulse of the Profession, a lack of clear goals was reported as the most common reason (37 percent) for underperformance or project failure.

Not too long ago, I emceed an event for AARP (the American Association of Retired Persons). They've been a brand partner of mine for several years, because I love the way the organization is committed to empowering its members as they enter retirement and the next stage of their life—with educational programming, community outreach, group discounts, and much more. At the event, someone in the audience pointed out that most people just dig in at work and go through the motions of living without stopping to think about what they want out of life or what they're willing to put into it.

I said, "Damn right. That's why there are so many opportunities for those of us who take the time to honestly
assess our strengths and weaknesses, our assets and liabili-
ties."

I hear all the time from people who tell me they're not
happy, they're not fulfilled, they want to make some sort of
change, and I can tell they're looking to me to help them
find someone or something to blame. If they're honestly
looking for help and searching for answers, I put it back on
them. I tell them the reason they're not happy is because
they don't know what they're looking for. Happiness
doesn't just up and find you on its own. You've got to have
a clear idea of what happiness is—what *your* happiness is—
and get after it. You've got to step off that moving sidewalk
and set your own trail. This is a hard message for a lot of
people to hear. We like to think we've got it all figured out,
or that if we follow along on what I call The Path of How
Things Have Always Been Done it'll eventually take us
where we want to go.

But that's not usually the case. We like what comes easy.
But that doesn't always get us any closer to the happiness
we're looking to find. **One of the key drivers in life is
knowing what you want.** If you're fortunate enough to
be a parent, you might have noticed that your kids always
have their eyes on the prize. But as we get older, that clarity,
that focus, often begins to fade. We forget the *why* behind
the things we do and the choices we make. When I listen
to people tell me they're not happy or fulfilled, I always put
it back on them. I say, "Well, what do you want? What will

make you happy?" More often than not, they'll have no idea, or no ability to put what they want into words, because they haven't allowed themselves to think in this way. So I'll put it back on them again and tell them to get back to me when they've figured it all out. After all, happiness and fulfillment and all those elusive qualities we seek are like any of the tangible objectives we hold out in front of us. Think about it: **We can talk pretty specifically about making our first million, or getting the corner office, or being able to afford a dream vacation, so why don't we put the same amount of thought and energy into recognizing what it is we *truly* want in life?** Otherwise, you could be working hard and busting your ass but really have no idea where you're trying to go.

Here's another way to think of it: You need to dig a little deeper in your thinking, so the goal is not just about making your first million—it's about what you plan to do with all that money. It's not just about landing that sweet corner office—it's what you hope to accomplish once you're in a position of power. And it's not just about setting off on that dream vacation—it's about what you hope to discover about yourself, or the person you're traveling with, that will help to recharge your batteries and power your days going forward.

What do you really want out of life? One good way to help you figure this out is to sit down and write your own obituary. It sounds a little morbid, I know, but it's a great exercise. It forces you to think through what's important, how you'd like to be remembered, what kind of footprint you want to leave here on this earth. I write mine every ten years, and when I do, it helps to frame my days going forward. It gives me clarity and helps me to recognize where it is I want to go and how I mean to get there.

I know with me it took a good long while before it felt like I had this figured out. And it can change over time, too. When I was younger, I'd always been about making money—I had my hustles and my side hustles since I was a little kid. I saw dollar signs in every transaction, but that's all. I was constantly running these equations in my head, trying to decide if a job or a project or even a relationship was worth my time.

Wasn't until me and my boys had the idea to speak into the culture and create a fashion brand that was all about inclusion and inspiration that it felt to me like I was headed *toward* something, instead of just chasing paper.

Later on, I'd start to feel the same way about educating and empowering entrepreneurs to start their own businesses and realize their own visions, so I headed off in a whole new direction.

And after that, when I was trying to make sense of my own mortality, I found a next-level layer of passion and purpose to my days.

Once I found my *why,* I was good to go. Each time out, the moment I *understood* what I was doing and why I was doing it was the moment I was finally able to make something happen, so I want to spend some time on this as we lean into this book. I want to drive home the point that **our *why* is all-important.** It's what gets us out of bed each morning and keeps us grinding late into the night. It's our silent fuel—our *not-so-silent* fuel. It's everything. And yet you'd be amazed how many people are content to ride the same moving sidewalk as everyone else.

If you could be your own lighting director, going back to the motivation for light idea I shared at the beginning of this chapter, how would you light the scene you're currently playing? Where would you look to shine that light next?

Obviously, figuring out your *why* is on you. I can't answer that question for you—I can only push you to consider it. But if you want to learn to leverage the *powershift* principle, you need to get on that—and fast. You need to step back from your day-to-day and think about this, long and hard: **What do you really want out of life?** Where do you see yourself in five years, ten years, twenty years? Don't just take it from me; if you check out books from Tony Robbins, Tim Ferriss, or Robert Kiyosaki, it's no coincidence that they all talk about this a ton.

Maybe put it this way: If you could do one thing every day for the rest of your days, what would that one thing be?

What have you always wanted but been afraid to go after?

If you could choose your own legacy, how would you want to be remembered?

Frame the question in whatever way you need to in order to come up with an answer . . . remember, it's not the question that matters, it's the *answer*. So ask yourself the right question and have at least some idea in your head how you hope to go about answering it. Really, this is job one. **Understanding your *why* is the first step to the *powershift* you're hoping to put into play, to move the needle on your life and career in a meaningful way.**

Now, all of this *power of why* business is not original to me. I might have embraced this concept a long time ago without even realizing it, but I didn't use this terminology. I had heard of this concept a few times before, but it wasn't until I heard a TED Talk by Simon Sinek that I started to think like this. The way he framed it helped me jump-start this conversation with myself in a whole new way. He went on to write a great book on this subject called *Start with Why*, and when I read that I got even more clarity on what was driving me.

Here's my favorite line from that TED Talk: "People don't buy what you do. People buy *why* you do it."

Think about that. Think about the power in that one little distinction—it changes everything, right? But what it doesn't do is answer the question for you.

Why?

That's one only you can answer—you're the only person with the operating manual for you. If you're not quite sure how to go about it, I'd suggest you start by looking in the mirror. Got to be honest, first couple times I stared into the mirror, I didn't get a whole lot back, other than the fact that I was pretty damn good-looking. But seriously, it took me a while to figure out my *why*. Back when we first came up with the idea for FUBU, for example, I didn't really recognize it for what it was. Initially, I just thought of it as a business opportunity. I didn't look past the dollar signs. And yet I think I figured out the *why* even if I couldn't put it into words. After all, it was right there in the name of our company: For Us, By Us. Sure, I could have just named the brand after myself, like a lot of designers were doing at the time, but what was driving me was this desire to empower people. I wanted our clothes to be about *a culture,* not any one person, so out of that we put our mission into play— even if I wasn't totally aware what we were doing at the time.

A friend of mine helped me to realize this not too long ago. We sat down one night and got to talking. He said, "Got to tell you, D. You were always about helping people."

I appreciated the sentiment, but I didn't buy it. I said, "Nah, man. Wasn't always the case. Back in the day, I just wanted to dress people."

But he pushed back. He pointed out that when I was growing FUBU, I could have named the company after myself, like so many designers were doing in those days, but instead I came up with this inclusive name that was all about belonging. Then I went out and hired the entire neighborhood, setting them up for jobs and careers while showing that you shouldn't undervalue or under-represent community. Then he reminded me that my books were all about helping people reach their fullest potential, from *The Brand Within,* which helped readers discover the power in their personal brands, to *The Power of Broke,* which encouraged people to use all of their resources to make their ideas happen, even when it felt to them like they were up against it, to *Rise and Grind,* where I was trying to light a fire in people to get them charging, hard, in the right direction. Then he reminded me that at some point late in the game I'd shifted my focus from investing in my own company and my own brand to investing in *other* people, companies, and brands. With *Shark Tank,* I was all about helping to lift these entrepreneurs from all walks of life, from all over the country. And finally, as a presidential ambassador for entrepreneurship, and as a motivational speaker and online educator, I was teaching people around the globe to find pathways to starting their own businesses and living their lives on their own terms.

It's good to have friends who push you to see yourself as you really are. I was grateful for his comments—they got me to see my *why* for what it was: to empower others to hit their goals and live their dreams. Like I said, it took me a while to put this into words—maybe that was the reason why the first couple businesses I tried to start didn't really go anywhere.

Maybe I wasn't ready.

Maybe *you* haven't been ready. Maybe that's why you've reached for this book—to help you shift your power from excuses and inertia to forward momentum and action. And the first step is understanding why it is you do what you do, and how you might do it better, smarter, more efficiently . . . more *purposefully.*

Bottom line: The only way to shift power to your side

of the room, to take control of the conversation, is to understand your *why* and to keep it real. It's like that expression you used to hear all the time, a couple years back, "Keeping it 100"—a reminder to tell the whole truth about yourself and whatever it is you're about. To move about with integrity. To stand for something. This idea should be the foundation for everything you do. It's the story we tell the world about who we are and what we want to accomplish, and in order for that story to resonate it's got to be rooted in truth. **We need to know exactly where we stand before we tell the world exactly where we're going.**

With me, this ability came from my mother. She let me know by her example that I was meant to work hard and achieve big things. She also let me know that she expected me to walk a higher road than my friends and running buddies, and that the temptations waiting for us on the streets of our neighborhood were not for me.

So go ahead and gather some of the people you trust and admire in your life and start pushing one another to figure some of this stuff out. You know the people I mean—the ones who tell it like it is, the ones who work as hard as you, the ones as determined as you are to succeed and who don't need you in order to achieve success. Together you can stoke each other's fire and help one another see those things about yourselves you may have missed—because without understanding the *why* beneath your determination, you're just going through the motions, working up a sweat without really getting anywhere.

START TELLING YOUR OWN STORY

Our stories define us, announce us, move us forward.

When we launched FUBU, our story was embedded in our name—For Us, By Us. A lot of people have asked me just who the "us" was in our name. Many people assume "us" meant the black community, but really it included all of hip-hop culture. We were just a group of guys who loved hip-hop, making clothes for anyone else who loved hip-hop. We loved everything about the culture, the lifestyle, and our styles were meant to celebrate that. We were all about the hip-hop movement, our community, about standing up and being counted at a time when established clothing brands didn't want anything to do with us. Our clothes were hot, but it took more than just great designs to get our brand to pop. Customers came to our brand only after we put it out there that we were joined together in the same fight, a part of the same movement; that we were determined not to be denied and that we were inviting them to get in with us—and hey, as long as we were fighting a good fight, we might as well look *good*.

In other words, we weren't just selling shirts, or even a certain style. We were selling a story—and underneath that story, there was a sense of purpose, a sense of belonging.

Here's the thing: In each of these stories, deep down, there is also the *why*—that fundamental truth that tells us who we are and what we're about. It applies to businesses, to groups, to brands, to movements . . . to individuals.

When I moved on from FUBU and *powershifted* into the role of serial investor and entrepreneur, my story changed, but my *why* fundamentally stayed the same. The focus on building community and empowering others to feel good through the clothes on their backs shifted into helping people find the confidence they needed to drive their entrepreneurial spirit. It was the difference between *looking* good and *doing* good . . . but end of the day, it was *all* good. These days, I usually introduce myself as "The People's Shark"—my way of putting it out there that I'm working for the people who come to my lectures and workshops, the people who read my books or take any of my online classes. I'm all about lifting people up and helping them to identify opportunities or areas of strength they might never come to on their own—and if it works out that they're in a position to lift me up as well . . . that's great.

In just about everything I do, as a consumer and as an entrepreneur, I'm all about the story. That's where I place my focus and my reputation—because, let's face it, **in today's world, we all live or die by the stories we tell,** which is why we need to think about the stories that define our past before we can begin to take that next big step. After all, as Maya Angelou once said, "You can't really know where you are going until you know where you have been."

TAKE STOCK

Like I said, my *why* wasn't much when I was starting out. As a kid, it was just about making paper—I looked at everything as a kind of money play. If it was worth my time, if I thought I could make some money on a deal, I chased it. Otherwise I'd look away. Later on, when I got out of high school, my *why* had more to do with a mix of money and opportunity. If I saw a way to make some money *and* have a good time, I was all over it—that's one of the reasons I started selling merch at all those hip-hop shows. It was only later, once FUBU got going, that I became a little more selfless in my thinking, and my *why* was about building a business that could support me and my friends and maybe provide a sense of community or belonging for our customers.

Once I discovered my *why,* I went looking for my *how* . . . I started setting goals. For as long as I can remember, I've had a goal in mind. But these goals weren't just things I'd think about in the back of my mind. I'd actually write them down—it's something I started doing as a kid, after I'd read Napoleon Hill's book, and it's something I still do today—*every* day, in fact. Each morning, I wake up and read the goals I've set for the next six months and those that expire after one year, five years, and ten years. I close my eyes and visualize each goal, almost like I'm willing it into view. And even with my eyes closed, I'm able to clearly see where I am and where I need to be. Lately, I've got a whole bunch of goals, and I break them down to my personal goals, about my health and relationships; professional goals, about where I want to be and the work I want to be doing; and financial goals, about the money I need to earn and set aside to allow me to live the life I want and take care of the people close to me. Some of my goals are general in nature—like, say, wanting to take care of my family and my employees. And some are very specific—like, say, wanting to cash a check for $102,345,086.32 by a certain date.

Just to be clear, the goals I actually write down and read aloud to myself are very specific. The ones I internalize—like, say, the hopes and dreams I have for myself and my family—are a little more general in nature.

(BTW, that's an actual number I wrote down with all my other goals, as a way to visualize what I wanted in a way that seemed real, not arbitrary, and when I shared that number in my last book I got a ton of comments from readers wanting to know what was up with me, going down to the penny like that. The answer: I'd rather hit a specific target than aim for a general area—that's why the bull's-eye is worth more than all those other rings on the target.) If you want to learn more about my goal-setting process, check out DaymondJohn.com/PowershiftExtras.

Most people don't do the kind of goal-setting we need to do in order to move ourselves forward. I've talked about this a lot over the years. I've written about this type of goal-setting, lectured about it, tweeted and 'grammed about it. It's an essential tool, and one of the reasons people tend to ignore it is because they don't take the time to think about their *why*.

So, tell me, what's your motivation for light? You gotta get real about your *why* before you can figure out your *how*. Wasn't always this way, though—at least not for me. When I was younger, the goal might have been to scrape together enough money to travel to a hip-hop show in Baltimore, or to buy a van and start my own ride-sharing business in my neighborhood. Or maybe I was saving up to buy a Mother's Day present, or some kicks I'd been eyeballing. My goals weren't long-term, the way they are now. They were mostly about what I wanted in the moment. But I eventually learned that to achieve big things in life, you need to set big goals. It's as simple as that.

Where is your why? Where did it come from? How did you find it? Or, more to the point, how did it find you? Are you going to law school because your parents are both lawyers and it was always assumed you'd follow in their path? That's not really the most compelling motivation for light, is it? Are you hustling for tips at Red Lobster because there aren't a whole lot of other options available to you? Again, not the best foundation for success. When I was doing my thing at Red Lobster, and selling hip-hop merch on weekends, I wasn't exactly fueling my passion in any kind of sustaining way. My two loves back then were hip-hop and fashion, and it wasn't until I thought to combine the two that I really had one of those aha! type moments and my why became clear. In a lot of ways, it was like an old Reese's Peanut Butter Cup commercial, where you had the chocolate in one hand, the peanut butter in the other hand, but it's not until you put them both together that you realize you've got something special.

The thing about goals is, it's pretty clear when you've met them—they're right there in front of you. Either you've saved up enough to make a down payment on that house, or you haven't; either you've sold through your first order, or you haven't. The thing about this honest-assessment business, though, is it requires you to be just that—*honest* in the way you see yourself. That can be tough for a lot of people. I get that. **Sometimes we tell ourselves a story of how we hope to appear instead of how we truly are,** but the key to this *powershift* principle is that it's got to come from a legitimate place. You've got to have the goods, the integrity, the authenticity, the *influence* if you want to even begin thinking about turning a situation to your advantage.

I'll spend some time a bit later in these pages on what it means to make a strong impression and build the kind of influence you'll need to bring the power to your side of the table. For now, though, I just want to emphasize the importance of laying in the right foundation as you're figuring out where to put your energies.

Take Olympic skier Lindsey Vonn. Like all the people I sat down with for this book, she's the kind of person you meet and can't help but want to know more about how she views the world. And after she kindly agreed to let me pick her brain for this project, it was clear to me that she didn't become the all-time-winningest skier without setting her sights high, putting in countless hours in training, and studying the techniques of her idols. You better believe she understood her *why* and her *how*—going all the way back to when she was three or four years old.

Most people don't take the time to think about what goes into an Olympic career. I mean, we see these athletes every four years, and a lot of times their races or events are over in just a couple minutes, so we tend to lose sight of all the hard work and extreme dedication that go into just being there. What's their motivation? What resources do they need to tap into in order to step up to this stage? Do they know they have greatness within them before they even set off on this journey? Or is that something they learn about themselves along the way?

In case you don't know Lindsey's story, she set her mind on competing in the Salt Lake City Olympics at the age of nine or ten. Think about that for a moment: When most of her little friends were out skipping rope or riding their bicycles, she was laying the groundwork to be the best there ever was in a sport she'd already come to love. **What were *you* doing at nine years old?** Well, what Lindsey Vonn was doing was sitting down with her father and putting it out there that she wanted to ski in the Olympics—and together they made a plan to make it happen.

This wasn't one of those *I want to grow up to be an astronaut* type moments. This was real . . . and rooted in a plan to make it real. The Salt Lake City games were ten years away, and Lindsey was already killing it on the youth circuit. A lot of parents, they might stiff-arm a kid who comes at them with that kind of announcement, but her father was all over it, too. In a lot of ways, her *why* was his *why* as well, because he'd also dreamed of becoming a world champion skier, before a knee injury put an end to all that.

Because he'd also been a competitive skier, her father

was able to recognize that even at nine years old Lindsey had a level of passion and commitment to her sport that was beyond her years. In other words, she had enough of a rep in her own household to bring her father around to her side of the table on this, and together they drew up what they started calling their "ten-year plan," complete with road maps and budgets and spreadsheets and projected outcomes. One thing she said that kept ringing in my head long after we spoke was "it's not just looking at the goal in front of you, but the ten goals beyond that."

Every couple months, Lindsey and her father would take that paperwork and spread it out on the dining room table to see where they were. There were certain markers they had to hit, certain results they needed to achieve by a certain date, certain dollars they needed to save or raise, to make sure Lindsey's progression was where it needed to be. They looked at where she was in the rankings, what races were coming, which camps she needed to attend—and of course which of those they could afford.

When I heard this part of Lindsey's story, I thought immediately of the kitchen table in our house on Farmers Boulevard in Hollis, Queens. That's where I sat with my mother when she taught me how to sew. That's where I took some of those meals my mother left for me when she had to work and couldn't make it home in time for dinner. That's where I sat with my boys when we started making our very first tie-top hats, so it took me back.

In Lindsey's case, it didn't hurt that she was enormously talented and fearless and all that good stuff, but it takes more than skill and courage to make it to the top. It's not enough to simply announce that you want to make the US Olympic Ski Team—or that you want to design clothes for people like you and your friends who are maybe feeling a little disenfranchised and overlooked by the major clothing manufacturers and retailers, for that matter. If that was the case, everybody would be out there skiing their butts off or making some noise with their streetwear designs. There'd be no way to separate the people who go hard from the people who just say they go hard, the real deal from the wannabes.

No, **to achieve any goal, whatever it might be, you've got to lay in a foundation.** Remember earlier when I talked about the importance of writing down your goals? That goes for your actual plan for laying the foundation, too. A Harvard Business School study found that of the 14 percent of people in the study who had actual goals but hadn't written them down were ten times more likely to meet them than those who didn't have a clear idea of their goals. The 3 percent who had written out their goals and plans were three times more likely than those 14 percent, so don't just take it from me: You need to plan out that foundation, and then you need to get out there and lay it. You've got to put in the work—what I call making an impression. In other words, you've got to call attention to yourself, bring the world around to your way of thinking. (Make some noise!) At the same time, you've got to account for the fact that you'll face some competition along the way, and that they might have their eyes on the very same goals. Never forget, there will always be others reaching for the same things you want, and they'll be putting in the work, too. Don't look at this as a discouraging fact, though. Competition can actually be critically important in building your influence. According to *Top Dog: The Science of Winning and Losing* by Po Bronson and Ashley Merryman, competition can actually push you to be more creative and innovative. They compiled research from various sources and studies to discover that 25 percent of people react negatively to competition, 25 percent of people have a neutral feeling toward it, and 50 percent of people actually benefit from facing competition. So frame your attitude toward your competition in such a way that you become part of that 50 percent and let your competitors drive you to build your influence in an even more creative way than you originally planned. You've got to understand them and find a way to stand apart. And to do that, you've got to take inventory of your assets—and yourself—to make sure you have what you need.

When you're constantly taking inventory of yourself, you set it up so you're never landing too wide of the mark or falling too far short. If things aren't turning out the way you'd like, you can move immediately to set things right—kind of like when you make a wrong turn on a road trip. Wait too long to discover your mistake, and you might travel a hundred miles in the wrong direction; figure it out immediately and you can double back and course-correct and be back on your way.

LINDSEY VONN, on setting goals: "I'm a goal-oriented person. And when I reach one goal, well before I reach that goal, I have another goal in place. There's always a tier of goals I have that I want to accomplish. I'm always looking for the next thing, always looking to be better than I was before."

When you come up in the fashion industry, taking inventory is a big part of your focus, in a very literal sense. At FUBU, we were constantly looking at the goods we had on hand and finding just the right balance between supply and demand. If we had too many XLs in our warehouse, we'd have to find a way to unload them at closeout, at a steep discount, cutting into our profits. Conversely, if we didn't have enough XLs to meet demand on an item, we'd miss out on a bunch of sales.

For us as individuals, too, it's all about inventory. Seems like a no-brainer to me, and yet I'm always surprised at the number of people who don't take the time to reflect in this way. Ask yourself:

What assets do you already have on hand?

What skills or strengths do you need to develop?

Are there areas of your business or certain relationships demanding too much of your time?

Can you identify any potential partnerships or outside resources that might help you grow your game?

What are you afraid of if you fail, and why?

These are the kinds of questions we need to be asking ourselves, at all times, and we need to be truthful with our answers—because, let's face it, **when we sugarcoat the situation to make things seem better than they are, we're only lying to ourselves.**

One great lesson of this conversation with Lindsey Vonn is that you can't always go it alone. When you're a kid, especially, it helps to have someone in your life who can help you identify your *why* and find a way to reach for it—to put it into play, you know. With me, it was my mother. With Lindsey, it was her father.

Basically, you've got to build the machine to take you where you want to go—and to get you there ahead of everybody else. So think about it: Who do you know in your life who can stand as a kind of sounding board, to help you separate your impossible dreams from the ones within reach? Is there a parent, a teacher, an older sibling, maybe a favorite aunt you can confide in who might be in a position to help get you started on your path? Is there a colleague or supervisor on the job who might be in a position to get in with you on a goal, or support you in some way as you look to shift your power in some new direction?

When they're taking inventory, most people look at their contact list to see who they already know who might be in a position to help them. As strategies go, it's always a good idea to tap your personal and professional networks for a lead or an assist—but as long as we're on it, why not turn the tables on this question and ask yourself who you know who might benefit from *your* expertise? I've always believed that the good you put out into the world will come back to you on the bounce, and this is one way to inventory your assets that just might remind you that it's almost always better to give than to receive—and hey, you never know what can happen when everybody else has their hand out and you extend a helping hand instead.

The idea is to find someone in your life to support you, encourage you, brainstorm with you—and make an effort to do the same for them. Sometimes all we need is one other person to tell us there's some merit to whatever it is we've got in mind—so reach out and see what comes back to you.

THE SECRET SAUCE

Of course, not everyone figures out their *why* so early in life. Take Charlynda Scales, a woman I had the privilege of mentoring through a program sponsored by Bob Evans Farms called Our Farm Salutes, giving a much-deserved assist to service members looking to make it as entrepreneurs. It's one of the top veterans-only grant programs in the country, and I've been excited to take part in it each year since its inception because it encourages our vets to tap the skills they've built throughout their military service and attach them to some goal or mission in the business world.

Sometimes you devote your life in service to others and

you need a bit of a push or a helping hand when you decide to transition into something new.

Charlynda was one of the first recipients of one of these grants, and it was an honor to mentor her as she launched her business—although, just being honest, it felt a lot of the time like *she* was guiding *me*.

A little back story: Charlynda's a fourth-generation service member. Her family has served in every branch except the Coast Guard, so this call to country and honor and discipline is baked into her DNA. She's a hard charger, determined to succeed, and when those qualities shine through it makes it easier to shift the power to your side of the table, to begin to make a name for yourself.

But determination alone doesn't mean success comes easy. You've still got to fight your way to the top, and it helps a whole lot if what you're fighting for excites you in some way—because, let's face it, **it's a whole lot easier to get up in the morning and work your tail off in service of a goal that really gets you going.**

CHARLYNDA, on the inspiration for her business: "There were three things in my grandfather's life he was passionate about. He was passionate about family. He was passionate about service. And he was passionate about sauce."

Yep, you read that right. *Sauce.* It was a big deal to Charlynda, because it was a big deal to her grandfather. You see, Charlynda's the CEO of Mutt's Sauce, a regional brand of special sauces that have become hot items in and around Ohio and parts of the Midwest. Her signature product comes from a recipe that was a closely guarded family secret for over fifty years. The trouble with those closely guarded secrets, however, is that people don't share them with anybody. That appeared to be the case here, when Charlynda's grandfather Charlie Ferrell, Jr., known as "Mutt" to friends and family, died at the age of seventy-one.

Mutt's death was a sadness on top of a sadness, because his sauce had been a constant in the life of his family. It was at every meal, always in the fridge, and Charlynda's aunts and uncles and cousins used it to dress up everything from everyday meals to special occasions. You could use it in place of ketchup or salad dressing or pasta sauce. It's even been used in a winning recipe in a Bloody Mary contest, so there's no telling how else people might enjoy the stuff.

When her grandfather died, Charlynda remembers sitting with her mother, feeling sad about the fact that his sauce had apparently died with him. "It was like losing him twice," she says now, but Charlynda's mother took her aside and gave her a gift that would change her life. It was Mutt's recipe. Just before he died, he'd set it on a piece of paper and asked that it be handed down to his granddaughter. It was the only time in his life he ever wrote it down, and Charlynda took it as a kind of sign. That's when she decided that she would make it her mission to put a bottle of her grandfather's sauce on every American table.

It went way beyond the sauce, with Charlynda and her grandfather. They had an unshakable bond. At Charlynda's commission ceremony, Mutt was the first person to salute her—that's what they call a Silver Dollar Salute in the military, and when that first person happens to be your grandfather who also served in the US Air Force . . . well, it's over-the-top.

Up until this time, Charlynda's plan had been to live a full military life and log her twenty years of service. That's how she saw herself whenever she looked in the mirror—but then, one day, she looked in the mirror and saw something different. She started to look at this recipe as a window onto something new. More and more, she started seeing that *something new* as a journey of purpose. But before setting off on that journey, she'd have to make the kind of *powershift* she hadn't been expecting, on both a personal level and a professional level.

CHARLYNDA, on *why* she does what she does: "Because my grandfather sacrificed so much for his family. Because I'm fourth-generation military, and that means something. Because my mother gave up everything so I could get an education. Because everything is connected and things happen for a reason. I tell people all the time they need to spend some time understanding that reason, to harness that *why*, so that they can know their purpose. To feel empowered by the good and the bad."

One of her first steps was to tap into a support network for aspiring entrepreneurs, where she was teamed with a mentor. When the mentor asked Charlynda what kind of business she wanted to grow from her grandfather's sauce, she didn't really have an answer. She wasn't prepared to give up her military career just yet, and at the same time she didn't want to phone it in as an entrepreneur. That's always a red flag when we hear a pitch on *Shark Tank* and try to determine whether or not a person is serious about growing their business. If they're not prepared to devote their full attention to their business, how can they expect one of us Sharks to work with them on it? Careful viewers of *Shark Tank* will note that one of the things I always tell the entrepreneurs on the show is not to quit their day job, but I don't think my message here is inconsistent. On the one hand, you don't want to cut off your income stream until you've got another one to replace it, but at the same time it might be hard to demonstrate to an investor or a potential partner that you're fully committed to a new business or product until and unless you're fully committed to it. So when Charlynda answered honestly that she wasn't quite sure where she wanted to take this business, and on what kind of timetable, her mentor answered with a great line I'm happy to pinch here.

He said, "We'll just move at the speed of determination."

I heard that and thought it was a great line because **no business or product or idea can grow any faster than our determination to make it happen.** But at the same time, if you hear it the wrong way, it's the kind of message that can give an aspiring entrepreneur an easy out. I mean, the last thing you want is for someone to think they can tackle their to-do list whenever they get around to it. If you hear it a certain way, it sounds soft, wishy-washy—almost like you're working with a built-in set of excuses if things don't go the way you've planned.

But one thing you should know about Charlynda: She's not soft or wishy-washy. She's not looking for excuses. She took these words and found the determination she'd been looking for all along—to honor her family and her grandfather's memory, and to shake things up in the special sauce aisle. She wasn't ready to leave her military career just yet, but she knew she had to work this business with everything she had while she was still on active duty.

By the time she applied for the Our Farm Salutes grant, she'd come up with a name for her grandfather's sauce, designed the label and packaging, and started filling bottles by hand and placing them in local stores. She guesses she was doing thirty to forty thousand dollars in annual sales, while continuing to serve in the air force, but she kept bumping up against a growth ceiling because whenever she'd make a major contact and see a possible way in to a major chain, she'd hear that she was too small to support a major order.

She'd found her *why*, but was stuck in getting to the *how*. So, like a lot of aspiring entrepreneurs, she looked to *Shark Tank*—or I should say, *Shark Tank* looked to her, as you'll see a little later on in these pages.

QUESTIONS TO ASK YOURSELF
AS YOU SHIFT YOUR POWER FORWARD

Okay, so you've got the *why* down—or, at least, you're working on it.

Now what?

Well, one of the things I find tremendously useful when I need to get real with myself is to do it in front of a mirror. Out loud. A lot of people, they have these conversations running through their heads all the time, about what they should be doing, what they shouldn't be doing. But silent doesn't cut it. Thoughts alone don't cut it. That's not the way we negotiate with our bosses, our partners, our friends and family, our opposite numbers in a deal, so it makes no sense to me that we should go about it any differently when we're looking to shake things up on our own.

Basically, we've got to take some sort of action to make our wishes come true, and the best way to start in is to give them voice. Think them through. Stare yourself down. Look long and hard into your own eyes, with confidence, and put those wishes out there—but don't call them *wishes.* Call them *goals* instead. *Wishes* are the stuff of dreams. They strip us of the power to make them so. *Goals* are the stuff of reality. They give us something to shoot for. So go ahead and sit yourself down in front of a mirror and ask yourself these questions—and know that it's what you do with the answers that will come to define you. Now I really want you to take the time to think through the following questions and provide real, specific answers for them. If you need some additional help, definitely check out the workbook at DaymondJohn.com/PowershiftExtras, because it frames them in an actionable way that can support your pursuit of your goals.

1. What do you want out of life?

Most people waffle on this one. It seems like the simplest question, but actually it's the toughest one to answer honestly. When we ask ourselves what we're passionate about, what we want to make happen, we tend to fumble for an answer. Or we reach for the obvious. It's like we're afraid to put our true goals out into the universe, because if we acknowledge where we want to go and still can't quite get there it might start to feel like we're some kind of failure. But the failure comes when you don't identify or articulate what you want, because you'll never hit the targets you can't see.

2. What do you *really* want out of life?

This is a necessary follow-up to our opening question, because I've found that the knee-jerk answer to the opening question is usually bullshit ... at first. It's only when we're pushed to be completely honest with ourselves, about what it is we want and how we plan to get it, that we can fire up the engines and think about making a meaningful *powershift* in pursuit. So don't give yourself the safe answer here. Don't tell yourself what you think you want to hear. Dig deep and tell it like it is. That thing you dare not mention? Go ahead and mention it ... and go for it!

3. Is there any one thing about your life you'd like to change?

Don't know about you, but I'm super-critical of myself, almost to a fault. On a purely micro level, every night when I look at my goals, I think, rethink, second-guess, worry. Every night when I look at my goals, I think back on the day and look at some of the things I might have done a little differently. Actually, that's a bit of an understatement: I look at all the things I might have done differently. I break down the day, hour by hour, looking for conversations that might have gone better, decisions I'd like to unmake, whatever. It's embarrassing to screw up, right? In some cases, it might even be humiliating, especially if we have to cop to that screwup in front of others. But my thing is to find a way to own my mistakes, to be the first one in the office to put it out there that I might have let everyone down—and then to let it be known that I mean to change. Immediately. There's no shame in doubling down on your commitment to do better. The shame comes in recognizing your mistakes and not doing anything about them. So, on a macro level, instead of beating yourself into the ground over your mistakes, let these experiences point you to areas of growth and change.

4. If you could set one achievable goal for tomorrow, what would it be?

Again, you need to be honest with yourself. And specific. We tell ourselves all kinds of self-limiting stories, but here the idea is to fill our heads with a self-empowering objective. Just one. If there's a difficult conversation you've been putting off, step away from the mirror and set it in motion. Right now. Hesitation can kill your forward progress before you even get going, so try to visualize the outcome you want and work backward. Send a text or an email to the other person and let them know you need to talk to them tomorrow—that way, you'll be less likely to give yourself an out. If your goal is to hit the gym first thing in the morning, leave your gear by the front door, maybe with a Post-it note over the knob saying, "No excuses!" Whatever it is, break through the barriers you've put in place that keep you from getting it done.

5. What is stopping you from achieving that goal?

Those stories I just mentioned? We should really call them self-defeating stories, because when we put a cap on what's possible we close ourselves off to all kinds of possibilities. Instead of telling yourself what you can't do, focus on what you can do. And if it works out that a lack of motivation or determination isn't stopping you, figure out what *is* wrong in your approach and come at your target in a whole new way. This is where those stories we tell ourselves can derail us. But if we find a way to highlight the positive, and break the process down to its component parts, we can bring a long-term objective into immediate view. It's a whole lot easier to start in with the reaching when you keep your focus on what's within reach.

6. What are you doing to make sure you're in a position to act when the next opportunity arises?

We've all missed out on something we wanted, right? But what sucks, really and truly, is when we miss out on something because we couldn't find the will or the fire to move toward it. When we become content with what we have instead of what we want, we close ourselves off from getting what we deserve ... so while you're looking in the mirror, why not put all those missed opportunities in the rearview and try to learn from them? Let an opportunity pass a single time, and it's a teachable moment. Let it pass a second time, and the moment might just be forever out of reach. So go ahead and identify a moment you'd like to have back. Then imagine that moment is at hand— how are you planning to shift the power now to where you're able to handle it and get the job done?

7. Tell yourself why you deserve this opportunity.

Go ahead and make the case for yourself. Set aside the self-limiting beliefs that tend to drag each of us down and blow some serious smoke your own way— because, hey, if you're not able to sing your own praises, how the hell do you expect someone else to recognize what you've got to offer?

POWER FACT When I tell you about the power to be found in setting goals and writing them down and visualizing them, don't just take my word for it. There's a psychology professor named Dr. Gail Matthews at Dominican University who discovered that people who do these things on a regular basis are 42 percent more likely to meet their goals than those who don't.

PART I

INFLUENCE
Make an Impression

The first gear you want to establish when you're setting yourself up to bring about significant change in your life is learning to use your influence in a way that brings you closer to your goals. The idea is to develop a winning rep, a persona that will take you where you want to go. To shift your power, you need to be standing on a firm foundation, and without a winning reputation you'll find yourself standing on a bed of sand. The ground at your feet will be unsteady, uncertain, and you'll have a tough time getting the traction you need to shift on the fly. But if you build influence in such a way that people can't help but know what you're about and what you've accomplished, you'll be standing on solid ground. Make the right kind of noise, early on, and you'll put yourself in a great position to make your next big move.

Chapter 3

STAND FOR SOMETHING

Think about the influential people in your life.

Think about the people you read about and admire.

Think about all the great leaders and visionaries through-out history who have helped to change the world, in big ways and small.

I'm betting you can come up with a single word or phrase to describe each and every one of them, because when someone makes an impression it's almost always tied to a specific accomplishment or character trait or world view.

Abraham Lincoln was honest . . . Muhammad Ali could float like a butterfly and sting like a bee . . . Aretha Franklin was the "Queen of Soul." But you don't have to be iconic or famous to leave that kind of mark. Look around your neighborhood and you'll see hardworking, everyday people who make an impression in their own way—like one of my very first mentors, Mr. Tim, who owned the corner store down the street and showed me the ropes of running a small business. Mr. Tim had been through all sorts of obstacles in his business—like economic recessions, changes within the community, and much more. Just because the guy didn't wear a fancy suit or use big business terms didn't mean that I couldn't learn from him. He wasn't necessarily iconic to anyone else, but he definitely left his mark on me.

What we're responding to here is the way these people carried themselves out in the world—the personas that came to define them.

Me, I've had a bunch of different personas at different stages of my life—and as a result, I left a bunch of different impressions. When I was a kid growing up in Hollis, Queens, I stood apart from my friends in the neighborhood who weren't always making the best decisions. I was cut a different way, and my boys understood this about me. If they were driving around looking for trouble, they knew to drop me off before they found it. "You might want to bounce, Daymond," someone would say. "We'll catch up with you later."

Later on, they knew all about my hustles and my side hustles. I was always working, always looking for all these different ways to make money, so that became my thing. I'd rally my friends to help out, depending on what I had cooking, or I'd go it alone. For a while in there, I "worked" the flea market on Rockaway Boulevard, keeping an eye out for people trying to steal. If I saw something shady, I'd point it out to the vendors, and they'd be so grateful they'd usually give me a couple bucks. But then I gave that up; it was important to me to move about the neighborhood with integrity, to make my mother proud, but at the same time I didn't want to be seen as a snitch. I needed to roll with my boys, you know. I wanted to be cool. Looking back, I can see that it doesn't paint me in the best light, the way I refused to rat out my friends, but I hope you'll consider the context. My definition of *cool* might have been different back then, but in my neighborhood, in my crowd, there was always some kind of trouble to be made, and it wasn't up to me to blow the whistle on my friends. The code of the streets said I could do right by myself, but at the same time I had to do right by my crew—and if that meant leaving it to someone else to catch them in the act of whatever it was they were up to, that's the way things fell.

Yeah, I was a mixed bag in terms of ethics—and I definitely don't think this same way today—but this was my hard-won set of principles. This was me, doing right by my mother and the values she instilled in me, while at the same time doing right by my friends.

What I'm getting at here is that the way we live our lives tells a story. At any given moment, we are walking advertisements for ourselves. Whether we know it or not, *whether we mean to or not,* we're constantly putting it out there what we're about, what's important to us, and what we hope to accomplish. Over time, if we're diligent and persistent and all that good stuff, people come to know us by what we've done in the past—and by what they can expect from us in the future. Maybe they know us as a good athlete, a hard worker, a loyal friend. Maybe they know us as someone who doesn't drink or do drugs, someone who's ambitious, someone who's true to their word. Whatever it is, our reputation attaches to us in a fundamental way and becomes not only part of the story we tell about ourselves, but part of the story other people tell about us.

I've thought about this a lot, and I've come to the conclusion that our ability to shift power in our favor starts with how we present ourselves to the world, and how the world looks back on us.

So tell me: What message about yourself are you putting out to the world?

What is the story everyone else is telling about *you*—especially when you're not around?

FIND YOUR CALLING CARD

Let's check back in with Charlynda Scales and her special sauce.

Before we'd ever met, Charlynda knew who I was. This alone isn't surprising when you work in front of the cameras on a prime-time television show, and when you make a name for yourself on the back of that show as a serial entrepreneur and motivational speaker. Charlynda had read my books, and she believed our stories were connected.

We'd both been raised by single mothers. **We'd both been taught to do and think and advocate for ourselves—essential building blocks when you're just starting out and trying to earn a living *and* a reputation.**

Six months after launching her business, in the summer of 2014, Charlynda got a call to appear on *Shark Tank*. The call didn't come out of the blue—she'd been encouraged to apply, never thinking she'd make the cut, but in those days our producers were looking to highlight strong veteran entrepreneurs. It made for good television, because there was usually a compelling story underneath the pitch, and because active-duty military members tended to do well in the Tank. They were used to being grilled and being made to answer for their actions.

When she flew out to Los Angeles for the taping, Charlynda got it in her head that I'd be all over Mutt's Sauce. She felt this deep connection, based on our histories and the vibe she'd gotten from my books. Problem was, I wasn't scheduled to be on the show for that episode. Back then, most of us regular Sharks sat out an episode every here and there to lend a little variety to the makeup of our panel, and to allow room in the Tank for an occasional Guest Shark, and here it just worked out that I was the one sitting out the day Charlynda came to pitch her sauce.

By the time she made it onto the set, she was a little flustered by the whole experience. The Sharks dug her sauce, but her answers to questions about her commitment to the business were nowhere near as crisp or polished as they needed to be. In the end, she didn't get an offer, and her segment never made it to air, so I had no idea our paths had nearly crossed when we finally met later on, as mentor–mentee.

Turned out that Charlynda's misfire on *Shark Tank* only fueled her resolve, so rather than letting it set her back, she doubled down on her mission to get her grandfather's sauce on every kitchen table. She used the twenty-five-thousand-dollar grant from that Bob Evans Our Farm Salutes program to step up production, and I'm proud to report that Mutt's Sauce is now being sold at Kroger supermarkets across Ohio, and Charlynda has increased production from seven hundred bottles per batch to twenty-four thousand, in four different flavors.

One of the great takeaways when I think about the path Charlynda is on is how it matches up to mine. Nothing was ever handed to her ... except for this recipe! And she doesn't seem to take anything for granted. It might have taken her a couple years to *powershift* from the air force to managing six-figure budgets, authorizing major expenditures, and selling boatloads of her grandfather's special sauce, but she moved with purpose and precision in pursuit of her goal.

So what does Charlynda stand for? What's the story she's putting out into the world? Right now, she's all about family, and service, and commitment. And here's the thing: Once you meet her and get to talking, you'll see that this has been her persona all along. She's also about hard work and sacrifice—been that way her whole life, too. Yeah, her sauce is delicious and unique and all that good stuff, but what stands out about her company is her pledge to honor her grandfather's legacy. And as Charlynda sets off to make an impression and build the kind of influence she'll need to continue to grow her business, that is her calling card.

What is your calling card going to be?

(Now go ahead and actually write this down so you can think through it.) Or check out the workbook at Daymond John.com/PowershiftExtras to keep track of that calling card.

BUILD THE BRAND, BE THE BRAND

I have a theory: The ways we build and develop our reputations are a whole lot like the ways companies market and develop their products.

In my work consulting for some of the biggest and best-known brands in the world, I've identified four stages of brand evolution that apply to every product and business. I first came up with this concept as I was trying to make sense of our breakout success with FUBU, back when we were working to take our brand to the next level. But what I eventually found as I looked at the marketplace in this way was that these four stages were not unique to our experiences at FUBU. They were the same for just about every kind of brand or company, across the board—and on a personal level, we go through them on our career paths and in our relationships as well. The way it works is, you have to pass through one stage in order to get to the next one—meaning, you know, you've got to work your way to the top.

I don't care how much money you've got to throw at a new enterprise, or how many years of experience you've banked, or how many powerful connections you have, if you think you can hit the ground running in whatever you're looking to do next, it's not gonna happen. No, you need to work your way through these stages one at a time (don't pass Go!), and you need to stick it out at each stage until the marketplace tells you you're good and ready to move on. I went through each stage with FUBU, and then I went through each of them again personally after I became a part of the *Shark Tank* family and repositioned myself as a serial investor, entrepreneur, and motivational speaker.

If you reached for this book looking for ways to make a powerful change in your life or career, I'm betting you can probably recognize which of these stages you're currently at.

The four stages:

Let's break them down ...

In the retail world, an **ITEM** is something generic—it's a notebook you might buy at the stationery store, say, or a sleeve of plastic cups for a party, or a nothing-special sweat-shirt you pick up on your travels because you forgot to pack one and it's cold. It's basic, simple, functional, and it fills an immediate need, and when you're out there shopping for it you're not looking for a name product or even a specific design, even if you know there are recognizable brand names in that category. You're just out to grab what you need, at a price that makes sense.

Next is the **LABEL** stage, where your purchase still isn't driven by the name on the label, but there's a name there just the same. I'm thinking here of the "house brand" labels you might see at Costco (Kirkland) or Home Depot (Behr) or Whole Foods (365). Yes, somebody took the time to sew a label on those clothes or slap a logo on the packaging and there might even be some in-store display meant to reinforce it, but you don't really notice it because your purchase has nothing to do with brand loyalty and everything to do with price and convenience. Maybe you're buying something you didn't really think you needed before you headed out to the store. Or maybe you've considered a name-brand alternative, but you're drawn to the price or apparent quality of this placeholder-type label. Whatever the case, the brand isn't *memorable,* and it's not likely you'll go looking for the same label again, unless of course you find yourself in the same store again, under these same circumstances.

After that comes **BRAND** territory—and in fashion, this is where most designers top out. **A brand is a name you recognize or have come to trust,** a name you associate with some distinct quality, like reliability, or sleek design, or made from all recycled products. It may cost more, but you're conditioned to expect a certain level of quality, or perhaps a distinctive style, that you might not look for in a simple item or generic label. If you're satisfied with your purchase and your experience, you'll probably seek out the same product or experience a second time. You might even recommend the brand to a friend, knowing that you can count on it to deliver a certain level of quality and value.

Finally, after developing that kind of brand loyalty in a customer, and growing it over time, brands reach what I call the **LIFESTYLE** category. This is the top of the heap, as good as it gets. It's the next-level success you see when a customer begins to identify with the world a brand has created, across a range of products and services. What you're selling, at this level, is an experience, a certain vibe, a sense of belonging. Under Armour, for example, started out as a simple T-shirt designed to wick away moisture when you wore it underneath your football jersey, but it's grown to include a full portfolio of leisure clothing, athletic shoes, and other fitness-related items. Tiffany, Victoria's Secret, Disney . . . same deal. They started small, usually selling one or two basic items or services, and grew into something much, much bigger—way beyond what their founders could have ever imagined. And in the case of Under Armour, way beyond the one-and-only product that set everything in motion—a product that was never even meant to be *seen* outside the locker room. I'll get to how this four-stage branding process can apply to you as a person in just a few pages.

FIND YOUR COMMUNITY

This is the path we followed at FUBU, but the funny thing is that we never set out to become a lifestyle—no, we just wanted to sell some threads. In the beginning, I was slinging tie-top hats and T-shirts from a duffel bag outside the Coliseum Mall in Queens, and it was only after I'd been at it a while and brought my boys into the business that we came up with a name and started sewing a label into our products.

A lot of thought went into our name, by the way, but what a lot of people don't know is that the meaning behind it was never really spelled out, except for one time very early on. This was somewhere around 1992–93, when I dug deep and took a booth at Black Expo in Manhattan. I'd been going to Black Expo for years, to get a jump-start on new product or maybe to pinch a couple ideas for the clothes I wanted to design. It was more a consumer show than a trade show—meaning, you know, it was open to the public and people would come in looking for deals.

At Black Expo, just like you see at other trade shows and conventions, the bigger the company, the bigger and more pimped-out the booth. We'd only been doing our FUBU thing for a couple months, so our booth looked more like something you'd find at a high school science fair. Still, I slapped a couple tables together and tried to make it look halfway decent and had a friend spray-paint a graffiti-style backdrop to punch up our display. The main item we were selling was our signature FUBU shirt—the only product we ever made that spelled out our story. It had our name on the front, printed in dictionary-style so people would know how to pronounce it, and on the back we wrote out our tagline: FOR US, BY US.

That's who we were, what we stood for, and word got around. **People started to know who we were, and they really responded to the story behind our clothes, so our name started to catch on.** You have to realize, back then there was no such thing as *going viral*. There was only word-of-mouth. Looking back, it's like we were watching a laser light show on a black-and-white television, but this was what we knew, how the game was played. What we were doing, really, was building community, even if there was no strategy behind the effort early on. We couldn't really see beyond the dollar signs that came with each sale. And yet within a couple years, through a variety of licensing deals, our FUBU name could be found on watches, fragrances, bedding . . . even music. What was so amazing about our growth into all these other areas was that it happened in an authentic way. If we'd set out to become this far-reaching lifestyle company, with products you could find on every floor of your local department store, we would have fallen flat on our faces. It would have been a case of reaching for too much, too soon, and trying to do too many things without ever really doing one thing well. The way it wound up happening had so much more validity to it, because it was a process. We earned the loyalty of our customers at every step of the way. Once they trusted us to help them look good in the clubs, they trusted us to help them look good at work, to smell good when they were out on a date, to feel good when they hit the sheets. The key to our success, really, was that we never tried to do too much or be too much all at once.

We'd just moved from *item* to *label* and were laying in the kind of foundation we'd need to become a meaningful *brand*.

We each have our own take, our own way to move ourselves from where we are to where we want to be. Me, once I identified this *item–label–brand–lifestyle* evolution, I spent a lot of time studying it, looking at how companies have grown their brands, and what I've found over the years is that it helps me to understand where I stand at any given time. I'm not the only one interested in the branding process. I have an entire department at The Shark Group dedicated to helping companies move up to the "lifestyle" category. It feels to me like the flip side of that line I always heard growing up that said, "To whom much is given, much is expected." First time I heard that, it filled me with this great sense of responsibility. It was like a charge . . . a *challenge*. We didn't have much, me and my mother, but we had everything we needed. By the standards of my neighborhood, we were damn near rich, so I knew at an early age to count my blessings . . . and never to take those blessings for granted.

You know, all these years, I never knew the source of that line, so when I wanted to mention it here in this book I went looking online to make sure I had it right. Turns out it's a verse from the Book of Luke, so I might as well quote it directly: "From everyone who has been given much,

much will be demanded; and from the one who has been entrusted with much, much more will be asked."

Words to live by, right? But in this context, I want to throw some caution at these words, because we need to keep our goals within reach—to train ourselves not to expect too much, too soon from the stuff of our dreams. Yeah, think big, go for it, reach for the moon and stars, but don't set it up so that what you're seeking is always just out of reach. You'll be disappointed each time out. Better to hit these markers along the way and make a long steady climb to the top.

When I first started thinking about this progression, I never could have imagined the *powershift* that was out there waiting for me as I pivoted into *Shark Tank* mode. And yet the reason I was able to turn this network television opportunity into something entirely new—a career trajectory that had almost nothing to do with the world of fashion where I had made a name for myself—was because I'd been through these four stages myself. FUBU's growing pains, as we moved from *item* to *label* to *brand* to *lifestyle,* were mine as well. **When we started out, nobody knew who I was, outside of my circle of friends and running buddies.** I was just a kid from the neighborhood selling merch, hustling—no different from a dozen other guys outside the same venue, from the same place, doing the same thing. But then our designs started to pop, and as people came to know the FUBU name they came to know mine as well. Together with Keith, J, and Carl, I was the face of the brand, and it got to where I did enough media interviews and walked enough red carpets that people started to know me. We had real, authentic credibility in the hip-hop community. Artists were featuring our clothes in their music videos, back when music videos still mattered.

We were making noise (most of it good, but I'll admit, we had failures, too) and some of that noise stuck to me, so when the time came for me to try to shift a little bit of power my way and slide into this new phase in my career, I was good and ready.

Okay, so maybe you're thinking this *item–label–brand–lifestyle* theory makes sense, but you're not convinced that it can apply to an individual—or, getting specific here, that it can apply to *you*. I mean, very few of us have marketing budgets earmarked for building out our personal brands!

The example I used in my book *The Brand Within* to illustrate the ways an individual can cycle through these same four stages was one of my heroes growing up: Evel Knievel. Actually, his real name was Robert Craig Knievel, but nobody really knew who he was back when he was starting out. Soon he was turning a bunch of heads whenever he pulled one of his stunts. He was *that guy,* the one people would stop and watch when he tried to jump his motorcycle over a bunch of stuff, across what seemed to be impossible distances. After a while, people started to point in recognition, and maybe even know his name. (It turned out Robert Craig Knievel wasn't a very good name for a daredevil, though, so when a cop slapped his nickname on him after he'd been arrested for reckless driving, mostly because it rhymed, it kind of stuck.)

Soon Evel Knievel was participating in local rodeos and ski-jumping events in Montana, and by the time he joined the army in the late 1950s, he'd moved from *item* to *label*—in other words, his reputation started to precede him. He went from being *that guy* to *That Guy,* in caps, and it could have ended there for him, but he kept at it.

When he left the service, he had the idea to start a kind of stunt show, pulling together a bunch of daredevil performers and billing himself as the main attraction, attempting bigger and more dangerous motorcycle jumps each time out, and the Evel Knievel name began to develop into a *brand*.

When I started paying attention to him, Evel Knievel had been at it for over a decade, becoming a kind of icon of flash and showmanship and fearlessness. We were always checking out his crazy stunts on *Wide World of Sports.* One of the things I noticed about Evel was that you never saw him out in public wearing anything but one of his glitzy motocross-type suits, which were usually done up in red, white, and blue. This was Evel in full-on *lifestyle* mode. **Even his name had become synonymous with a certain type of reckless behavior.** Whenever me and my boys found ourselves doing something wild or dangerous or stupid, we'd say we were "pulling an Evel Knievel"— that's how deeply his brand had been ingrained into the culture.

But Robert Craig Knievel didn't go from just some fearless, anonymous guy who liked to do wild stunts on his motorcycle to being this world-famous daredevil whose name alone could inspire a bunch of kids in Hollis, Queens, to do some crazy, fearless stunts of their own overnight. He got there incrementally—in stages. Same way you're probably looking to develop your own reputation and build influence in whatever it is you're out to do. Here's how (and for actionable ways to answer the following prompts, head over to DaymondJohn.com/PowershiftExtras):

1. Define who you are.

Put it into words. You don't have to say these words out loud or anything, but speak them to yourself until they sound just right. The idea here is to try them on for size, see if there's a good fit—just like Evel when he decided to try on a new moniker. Come up with a list of five or six adjectives that describe who you are—or at least the person you aspire to be: caring, diligent, resourceful, generous, rebellious, curious. Carry yourself with those words in mind, and they'll start to stick.

2. Figure out how to signal to others what you're about.

If you're all about kindness, be kind. If you're all about generosity, be generous. If you're all about hustle, hustle. Don't talk . . . *do*. And don't just do . . . *be*.

3. Make an effort to share your "brand" with others.

Understanding your brand and how you see yourself is important, but if you don't do anything to let the world see you in the same way you're just banging your head against the wall. You don't have to jump the Grand Canyon on your motorcycle to call attention to yourself—just look for opportunities to do your thing in a way that shines back on you. For example, if your company has a charitable mission tied to it, make sure you talk about that on your website or social media posts. If you want your co-workers to think of you as a caring, thoughtful person, make sure to write a letter to an employee every week about why you value them on your team. Make sure to share what makes your brand so special, so people can connect those thoughts to you.

4. Find a way to amplify that message.

Now go ahead and take that shine up a notch, but as you do remember that what might have worked for you in the year 2000 won't work quite so well in 2020. Can't imagine there are too many people still checking into your Myspace account, so find a way to get your message out there, while making sure you're also getting with the times.

5. Make a splash.

One of our first big marketing splashes at FUBU that put it out there to the fashion world that we had arrived was landing a display window at Macy's. But it wasn't just *any* display window, which of course was every up-and-coming designer's dream. No, the four of us—Keith, Carl, J, and me—climbed into the window ourselves and hung out in the window for a couple hours. As far as I know, nobody in hip-hop had ever done that before, and the reason nobody had ever done it was that nobody had ever thought to ask. We came up with the idea and put it on the table with the Macy's people, and they were all over it, so we were given the chance to tell our story in this unique way.

6. Revise your story.

No matter what we do or what persona we want to share, our focus changes over time. Our priorities, our personalities, our personal network ... they're constantly evolving. Your story should be changing, too, so find a way to hit the reset button every once in a while and make sure the person you've always aspired to be looks at least a little like the person you've become.

POWER FACT Keep it real. The power of making an authentic connection is all-important—doesn't matter if you're selling a product. How important? Well, according to a Zimmer Radio & Marketing Group report, 80 percent of social media users cite "authenticity of content" as the number one reason they choose to follow a company or brand, so take the hint.

Chapter 4

DEVELOP A CLEAR AND CONSISTENT MESSAGE

So why is the story we tell ourselves about who we are and what we do so important?

Because it puts it out there that we mean to be counted.

Because it announces to the world that our intentions and our principles match up with our methods.

Because it helps to position us for whatever comes next.

First order of business for anyone looking to build the kind of foundation that will set them up to *powershift* into their future is to spend some time on that story line—and then start telling the hell out of it. **Without a story underneath whatever it is we're making or selling or doing, we're just going through the motions.** We're generic, indistinguishable from our competitors. We're not establishing any kind of credibility or encouraging any kind of buy-in from the people we're hoping to reach with our efforts.

I call it **building influence** when we take the time to understand the communication channels we need to tap in order to signal what we're about. But here's something you need to keep in mind: **It's one thing to *walk the walk,* but it's quite another to let it be known that you're walking the walk.** What I mean by that is you need to find a way to *put it out there* that you're a person of integrity, passion, commitment . . . or whatever else you want to stand for. Find your two to five words that announce who you are and what you're about, and carry yourself accordingly. And keep in mind, those words don't all have to be positive, if that's not how you're wired. Just look at how Old Dirty Bastard announces himself to the world—he's an old, dirty bastard, and damn proud of it! And whatever you stand for, you need to own it. Because remember, while the stories we tell ourselves are incredibly important, the stories others tell about us are just as important.

What's interesting here is how the world has changed since FUBU came on the scene. Back then, we couldn't really control our narrative, the way young entrepreneurs are able to do today. We could sit for an interview with a local reporter and talk about how we were a black-owned company, how we were all friends from the neighborhood, how we loved hip-hop, all of that, but we couldn't actually write the story. We had no say as to how the paper would play it, what kind of headline they'd run, what photos they'd use. It was all out of our hands, so if we didn't like the coverage there wasn't really anything we could do about it. Now, if you're running a start-up or launching a new line, you can use your social media platforms to shape how your brand or your product are seen out in public, so that's a key shift, and I tell young entrepreneurs all the time to take good and full advantage of all the marketing tools at their fingertips. As long as you keep it genuine, as long as you're honest with your customers, you're good.

Think of it this way: Whatever message or persona you're putting out there, it's got to match up with your actions. That's what Lindsey Vonn was able to do so effectively when she transitioned first from the world of youth sports and club skiing onto the Olympic stage, and then from the very top of her sport into the world of business. If you followed her career you'll know that while she was out there piling up all those World Cup victories and fighting her way back from all those injuries, she was also establishing the fierce, no-quit, take-charge persona that eventually came to define her.

Obviously, it takes time for that kind of rep to take hold. It didn't happen right away, but over time people all over the world came to know Lindsey as a fearless competitor who wasn't about to let a bunch of injuries keep her down. From there, she became a head-turning star of her sport, someone sponsors wanted out there promoting their brands and products. So by the time she retired, she'd made her name synonymous with grit, guts, speed, determination, and the kind of relentless spirit you need to drive success in *any* arena, and she was able to build on that hard-won reputation and find a way to make it all work for her, even off the mountain.

That's how it goes with this *powershift* business: It's not an *add water and stir* deal. It's cumulative, gradual. It's about taking the time to develop a reputation that fits with the message you want to put out into the world—*and* it's about using that time to good and full advantage.

BE PREPARED TO REWRITE YOUR STORY

Got to tell you, back when we closed our manufacturing and distribution deal for FUBU I never imagined we'd have the success we did right out of the box. We blew up in response to a hole we saw in the marketplace, and we were blessed to be able to fill that hole and make a little bit of an impact in our community. Looking back, we were in *too much, too soon* territory. For the first time in our lives, we had money—like, serious money. Me and my boys, we were running around, going out, partying pretty hard. *Over-balling,* we used to call it. The money went straight from our pockets to our heads. We were spending like crazy: cars, real estate, Cristal, jewelry . . . All those zeros at the ends of our paychecks messed with our priorities, I think it's fair to say, and in my case they messed with the family I had just gotten around to starting—ended up separating me from my daughters and their mother, which just about knocked me on my ass.

And then when that flow of money started to slow down, even just a little bit, I began to see some trouble spots in our business plan. When we were riding high, we thought the money would last forever . . . that the upward trajectory we'd been on would keep trending that way . . . that whatever blessings had smiled down on us in the first place would keep on smiling. But that wasn't how things would go. (It almost never is!)

It was around then that I started spending a lot of time trying to identify the areas of strength I could maybe attach to other types of businesses and prospects beyond the world of fashion, and eventually I got involved in brand extensions and licensing agreements with a variety of players and products. This was me, trying to pivot, seeing if I could maybe start to tell a *different* story—or at least the next chapter of the same story. This was also around the time I began to think of *myself* as a kind of brand, above and beyond FUBU, so I started showing up more and more on shows like CNBC's *The Big Idea with Donny Deutsch,* where I started to get recognized as a commentator on brands, fashion, trends, and popular culture.

Understand, what I'm about to tell you isn't me blowing smoke my own way—but I started hearing from a lot of people back then that I was good on camera, fast on my feet, a quick study. Some of that positive feedback got me thinking about finding some kind of full-time outlet on television. Already I was looking at ways I might empower young entrepreneurs and maybe share some of what I'd learned getting FUBU going, and TV was really the only platform available to me at the time. This was back when the social media landscape was just taking shape, and people weren't doing podcasts or teaching online courses the way they are today, so TV and radio was where my head was at. I even started coming up with ideas for shows I wanted to develop. And so **if you'd pulled me aside in those days and asked me what I'd be doing five or ten years down the road, I would have said I'd become some type of on-air commentator or television producer**—because, already, I could see a way for me to tap the power of the medium as a way to amplify the power of whatever FUBU had come to represent.

One thing I want to make clear: When I was growing up, I never even imagined someday being on television. It was just so far removed from my experience, you know—beyond my imagination. Sewing tie-top hats and making T-shirts was a vision I could actually *see*. But my face in front of the camera, let alone in front of millions of people—the thought never even entered my head. But once FUBU started popping and I ended up promoting the brand with a bunch of interviews, I found that I was pretty comfortable in this kind of spotlight. **Turned out I was good at running my mouth, especially when I had something to say.** And I liked it, too. So I got to thinking, *Hey, maybe there's something to this television thing,* so I kept at it, started putting myself out there more and more.

And the more I got out there, the more I'd hear from people who found something useful in my story—because, of course, I wasn't *just* running my mouth. I was sharing my experiences, letting people know that if a dyslexic kid from Hollis, Queens, could find a way to build a global brand on his mother's kitchen table . . . well, then anything was possible. They liked all of those *Power of Broke* type elements to my story. And so I kept on looking for ways to speak into that experience.

That's pretty much where I was when *Shark Tank* came calling. I wouldn't have described it in this way at the time, but I can see now that it was a major *powershift* moment. My motivation for light at this stage in my life was pointing me in this direction. I was realizing that there weren't a whole lot of people of color who weren't rappers or athletes, speaking into the culture in this way, so I started to see this as my unique selling proposition. I'd gotten it in my head that it was time to move on to something new, and was writing down words like *television* and *broadcaster* and *analyst* on the running list of short-term and long-term goals I always had with me, although I didn't have a clear idea how to get from where I was to where I wanted to be. That all started to change when I heard from reality television producer Mark Burnett about this new show he was developing based on a hit British series called *Dragon's Den*—which was based on a hit Japanese series of the same name. There had also been a hit version of the show in Canada, so this American edition was going to be like the sixth or seventh go-round on the format. The idea of the show was to give aspiring entrepreneurs the chance to pitch their business concepts to a panel of well-known (and not-so-well-known) investors, and judging from the success of the show in these other markets, audiences seemed to really respond to it.

Suddenly, I found my unique selling proposition. I was a young hip person of color with a global brand and an entrepreneur, not an athlete or musician, and I could relate to the everyday person. And it turned out that Burnett saw something in me, something that viewers wanted.

I knew who Mark Burnett was, of course. *Survivor* was one of the biggest reality shows on television, and he was also killing it with *The Apprentice,* so the guy obviously knew his stuff—this was clear even to an outsider like me. Trouble was, I wasn't getting any of Mark's calls at first. In those days, I didn't have anyone on my team vetting any of these requests for my time or attention, so the messages on my answering machine would just pile up. I never really listened to them, because most of them were from stockbrokers or real estate brokers looking to rope me into some investment or other, so one of the great lessons from the early part of this *Shark Tank* story is this: Always listen to your voice mail.

Chances are, if you're reading this book, you already know the story of how *Shark Tank* jump-started the next phase of my career. But what you might not remember is that we struggled to find an audience those first couple seasons. Every year, it was a toss-up whether or not we'd be renewed. We started out airing in the summer, when viewership is traditionally down, so it took a while for us to find (and keep!) an audience. But hey, we were giving it our best shot. Each of us Sharks was out there promoting the show, working like crazy to push the partnerships we'd entered into on camera to some kind of success. While we were prepping and taping the pilot, I was also working on my own agenda, trying to find a platform where I could educate and empower entrepreneurs in a meaningful way. Since it wasn't clear to me just yet that *Shark Tank* would work out, I kept pushing for a meeting with Mark Burnett, so I could pitch my other ideas.

Got to be honest, the opportunity to get in a room with this TV icon had been one of the biggest draws as I looked at all the pros and cons of doing the show. Sure, there was the chance to try something new, to step from the urban fashion world and into a public light, to sharpen my image with a renewed focus on investing and entrepreneurship. But most of all there was the chance to sit down with the hottest producer in reality television and sell him on my ideas.

On the other hand, there was the uncertainty of not knowing if the show would be a hit or a miss, of having to spend my own money to invest in these start-up businesses based only on a brief sales pitch on a Hollywood sound-stage, of committing to a television gig that wasn't exactly offering me television money. Plus, I had no way to know whether or not people would take me seriously in this new role.

Turned out that I did finally get my meeting with Mark, right after we finished shooting the pilot. We met for breakfast at the Four Seasons, and he literally shot down all three of my ideas before the orange juice arrived.

So there was *that*. But there was also *this*: *Shark Tank* would go on to become one of the most successful business shows in American television history. My role on the show and the platform it provided would transform my career and stamp my days going forward. And all of that uncertainty would eventually fall away, allowing me to look back on the decision to join the cast as one of the essential *powershifts* of my life and career.

FACE REALITY

Like I wrote earlier, I never could have imagined this pivot into reality television. It was so far off the map that it was tough to spot the path from where I'd been with FUBU to where I wanted to be. The same could be said for my friend Kris Jenner, who'd made her own *powershift* into the world of reality television just a couple years earlier.

As you might know (if you haven't been hiding under a rock for the past dozen or so years), Kris is the matriarch of the Kardashian family, and the executive producer and star of the wildly successful show *Keeping Up with the Kardashians,* on the E! cable network. I'd known Kris for a couple years before the launch of the show—in fact, I knew the whole family. I got to know them through Kris's daughter Kim Kardashian, who I met through a fashion show for one of my brands—Heatherette. Then I met

Khloe Kardashian, who for a couple years was almost like a fifth member of our FUBU squad. She used to hang with us all the time and we had a blast together. I reached out to Kim and Khloe to see if I could get them and their sisters to wear some of our clothes, back in the very early days of product integration and social media influencing. **That had been one of the key drivers of our early successes at FUBU, getting prominent rappers and hip-hop artists to wear our clothes in their music videos.**

Nobody called it "influencer marketing" in those days, but that's what we were doing. And there was no denying its effectiveness, when you could find a star or even an emerging star and get them to promote your product. This kind of product integration had been going on since the early '90s in music videos, and for about ten years before that in the movie business—starting, most famously, with the deal The Hershey Company cut to have Reese's Pieces featured in a little movie called *E.T.*

(For those of you keeping score at home, that's the second product placement reference I've made in these pages on behalf of The Hershey Company. I don't plan on making any more the rest of the way, but if I do I should probably get a lifetime supply of chocolate, don't you think?)

Having really launched FUBU through strong product integration in music videos, I knew I could apply that same logic to TV, and there was a big opportunity with the Kardashians and their upcoming show. So I had Kim, Khloe, and the rest of the whole fam sporting one of my fashion brands, Coogi, throughout the entire first two seasons of *Keeping Up*.

The best thing was I also got additional exposure when they'd wear some of our stuff when they were out clubbing, or sharing pictures of themselves on Facebook or on this weird little platform nobody had truly figured out just yet called Twitter. Again, nobody was using the term *influencer* in those days, but it was clear to everyone that we were trading swag for eyeballs, which seemed pretty win–win to me; they got free stuff and we got exposure, and a certain amount of goodwill from the people who paid attention to the comings and goings of Khloe and her sisters.

At the time I'd been trying to help the girls get something going in New York, mostly on the fashion side of things, but in the end it was Kris, who just happened to be married to former Olympic gold medalist Bruce Jenner—now known as Caitlyn Jenner—who had the idea to invite a camera crew into their lives and let the world see how they lived. Kris had been acting as her daughters' manager for a while by this point, so she knew her way around a meeting room—and more to the point, she knew how to spot a good idea.

Kris tells me she sold the show in a quick-pitch to Ryan Seacrest and then the two of them shopped it around. Within thirty days, they'd sold the show to E! and started filming—before she and her family even had a chance to think if they had the kind of thick skin and strength of character to hold up under the constant scrutiny of a full-time camera crew. It was only later that she discovered she and her daughters were blessed with the skills and toughness they'd need to survive and thrive in the world of reality television they helped to create—but at the time, it was a full-on roll of the dice, which reminds us that sometimes you just have to take a chance and see where the deal takes you. "It happened so fast," Kris says, "there was hardly enough time to think about what we were getting into. It's like we jumped on a moving train we never saw coming."

I love Kris's moving train analogy here, because that's how it can feel when you make a leap from what you know to what you can only imagine. **The ground at your feet is no longer certain, but you know you've got to hop the train and just go for it.**

Unlike those first couple seasons of *Shark Tank*, *Keeping Up with the Kardashians* was an immediate hit, and Kris tells me it's like their lives were changed overnight. Her daughters had been well known in certain circles, and Kris herself was already a player in and around Hollywood, but all of a sudden she was moving about in the light of celebrity.

I don't think anyone in the Kardashian camp was prepared for the runaway success of *Keeping Up with the Kardashians*. To hear Kris tell it, it took a while before any of them recognized the show as the foundation for everything they would do going forward. For the first couple seasons, she says, it was more of a side business than a full-on enterprise. In a lot of ways, it was meant to be a fun little side something she and her family could all do together to make some money and maybe raise their profile until the next little side something came along.

But instead of serving as a springboard to the next big thing, the show *became* the next big thing . . . fast. It became the ultimate *powershift* for Kris and her daughters, because it kicked things up to a whole new level. And the reason the show popped the way it did was because it was so real. Sure, the flash and the style were the elements that tended to draw in viewers and capture headlines, but what kept people coming back to the show week after week were the raw emotions . . . the *heart*.

KRIS JENNER, on the *story* behind *Keeping Up with the Kardashians* and the emerging Kardashian brand: "We showed ourselves as we truly were. We showed our lives and our loves and shared the things that truly mattered to us, without filter. That's what people responded to, and all of a sudden people all over the world were really invested in us and what we were up to as a family. It changed everything."

Just how *real* do the Kardashians keep it on TV? Well, even though Kris and her family live their lives in front of the camera—24/7, or just about, when the show's in production—they've rarely asked the crew to power down during a difficult or private moment. And they've almost never exercised their creative control and left sensitive material on the cutting-room floor, either.

"If we did that, I don't think we'd have been this successful," Kris says. "Even if it's cringe-worthy, the idea is to show people as we truly are, so we try to honor that."

So tell me, are you keeping it real and living your life as if millions of people are watching you, 24/7?

FIND YOUR VOICE

With me and my fellow Sharks on *Shark Tank,* success was more of a slow roll. Our first season launched in August 2009, and I'll be honest, we weren't exactly lighting it up in the ratings right out of the gate. And I think I probably lost about $750,000 in the partnership and licensing deals I entered into during our first season—not exactly a good sign, but I told myself not to worry about the money. I'd lost money before—that comes with the territory when you're investing in other companies.

Part of the problem with our *Shark Tank* launch was that nobody knew what to make of us those first few seasons. Were we a game show? A reality show? A business show? Were we *really* investing our own money in some of these wild deals? There was nothing else like *Shark Tank* on TV in the United States, so there were no easy comparisons—which meant the aspiring entrepreneurs and innovators who appeared on the show didn't know what to expect out of the deal, either.

Over the years, of course, *Shark Tank* stayed on brand, consistent in its integrity and in its message while refining the ways we got that message out there. And through the thousands of entrepreneurs who have appeared on our show (and the tens of thousands who've applied), we have found our messengers. They're the true heart of the show. Taken together, their stories reveal a piece of the American dream in a way that shows the entrepreneurs in the studio (and at home!) that anything is possible. They've helped to position *Shark Tank* as a great proving ground and launching pad for new products and business concepts mixed with small business case studies, human interest stories, and unscripted drama where the personalities and relationships of the Sharks can shine through.

We found our "voice" as a show—and out of that, we were finally able to tell our story.

What are some of the ways you can get your story in alignment with your hopes and dreams (and don't just read the following prompts, head to DaymondJohn.com/PowershiftExtras to find ways to execute them)?

1. Drink your own Kool-Aid.

Whatever it is you're selling, you've got to buy it, too. That means being your own best customer. When you stand behind your product, your service, your mission, you project authenticity and make it easier for others to stand alongside. For example, for a time in there I pretty much wore FUBU products all the time, in order to put it out there that I was all about the brand and the brand was all about me. My boys were all doing the same thing. For a clothing line like ours, where the message behind it was all about inclusion and building a sense of community, this was critical.

2. Stay "on brand."

This is a kind of corollary to the "Kool-Aid" message above, but the difference here is that you can't let yourself stray from your narrative even for a moment. In other words, if you're out to sell "Kool-Aid," don't be caught out in public sipping from a "Hi-C" juice box. At FUBU we lived and breathed the message behind our clothes, and we only designed stuff we wanted to wear, so it all worked out—not in a by-the-book sort of way, and not by the letter of any contract, but because this was the image we wanted to represent.

3. Understand that your real impact will come over time.

Good stories take a while to tell. (Just look at *Game of Thrones*!) Don't be discouraged if you make a couple false starts, because they're inevitable. What's also inevitable is the slow build that finds most new businesses when they open their doors. Know that customers won't be beating a path to you on Day One. By the same token, careers don't blow up overnight. No one gets promoted up the ladder their first week on the job. Stay focused and keep doing your thing, building up a solid reputation for what you're putting out there, and good things will find you . . . eventually.

4. Look for others to join you or stand in support of your movement.

It's tough to go it alone, so why not get in with another like-minded soul and go through these motions together? When I launched FUBU, I had Keith, Carl, and J for support. When *Shark Tank* happened, I was out there with my fellow Sharks, and our entire production team, trying to promote the show and turn people on to what we were doing. Being a part of a team like this is a great way to share the many burdens that come with trying to work your way up. It's also a whole lot more fun.

5. Always be on the lookout for something new.

There's a life cycle to every business—and to every personal brand. Just look at how Oprah Winfrey morphed from a local television personality into a global icon of empowerment and integrity . . . how Bill Gates went from a tech guru to one of the richest men on the planet, and then from there building a legacy as a philanthropist and humanitarian . . . how Muhammad Ali started out a dynamic boxer from Louisville named Cassius Clay, won a gold medal at the Olympics at eighteen years old, converted to Islam, put his principles on the line to oppose the Vietnam War, and ended up as one of the most celebrated athletes and activists of all time. Successful people find a way to shift their power from one area to another. You can, too. No matter how great things are right now, you should always be prepared to make a *powershift* into the next opportunity—and it's better to make that move *before* you're up against it.

POWER FACT Can't hit this one hard enough: 94 percent of consumers say they're more likely to be loyal to a brand that is completely transparent in its marketing and promotion than to one that plays a little fast and loose with the truth. So get on message, and stay on message, and let's see what happens.

Source: Zimmer Radio & Marketing Group

Chapter 5

LOOK FOR POINTS
OF CONNECTION

I mentioned in the previous chapter how tough it can be to go it alone, and here I want to spend a little more time on this idea, because when you're looking to establish a reputation you've got to call a little bit of attention to yourself. After all, it doesn't really matter what you're putting out into the world if no one is watching.

Oh, and it's not enough *just* to get people watching—you've got to make a strong first impression (and second and third and one hundredth impression!) to bring them along to your way of thinking.

Influence is a two-way street: To make a good impression, you need to find ways to connect with

people, to make them feel seen. Don't know about you, but I find that one of the best ways to find common ground with someone is to put myself in that person's shoes. I'll think about what they might have going on at home, what they're hoping to get out of each day, where they want to go on their next vacation.

If I'm in a first meeting, one-on-one, I'll take some time before we get down to it to ask about that person's family. A lot of times, it works out that we'll have kids the same age, or we share a similar background. Maybe we listen to the same music or lean the same way politically. Maybe we're both wearing a Yankees hat. Whatever it is, however it comes up, it's a good idea to connect all these dots in such a way that the common ground at your feet feels right and good and true. It might just be that the common ground you find is literally the ground beneath your feet. Sometimes we're most comfortable pursuing opportunities where we're most comfortable. Did you know that in 2018, according to a *U.S. News & World Report* survey, roughly 80 percent of venture capital dollars invested in small businesses and start-ups went to just four states? What that tells me is that California, Massachusetts, New York, and Texas have not only become hotbeds for innovation and entrepreneurship, but that's also where like-minded people tend to find one another in pursuit of their shared goals. I'm not suggesting that you play things up and make it sound like you've suddenly found your new best friend, but you'd be amazed at how reassuring it can be to collaborate with someone with a shared point of view, even if it only applies to one particular aspect of your lives.

The more you get to know people, the more you learn about them, the more you can tap into their unique passions and goals and skill sets. That's what I did with each of my FUBU partners; I got to know what they loved doing—and were good at—and gave them responsibility in those areas. Keith, for example, has always been more social and outgoing, so he dealt with celebrities. J always focused on style, so he was in charge of keeping up with fashion, etc.

Learning who people are and what they are about also opens up opportunities to make these kinds of connections on a bigger scale. At FUBU, when we started working with Samsung, their Korean partners, and a number of other Asia-based companies we learned that their big thing was karaoke—that's how it is in a lot of Asian companies. It's a part of the culture. It doesn't matter if you're the chairman of the board or the kid in the mailroom, when there's a company-wide meeting or a dinner or whatever, you can bet there's going to be some singing involved. It's a great common denominator, a great way to level the playing field. Everybody's in the same boat, doing the same thing, cheering one another on.

So I learned to sing my little heart out every time our colleagues came in from Seoul—and it just worked out that our Empire State Building offices were smack in the middle of Koreatown, so there were dozens of karaoke bars in our neighborhood. When I went to Asia, same thing . . .

there was always karaoke, and out of that we were able to communicate with one another as equals. Hierarchy didn't matter. Talent didn't matter. It only mattered that you stepped onto that stage and sang. So we did.

There were points of connection to be found with my distribution partners Bruce and Norman individually as well. We shared the same office, but at first we didn't share a lot of points of reference. We came from such different backgrounds. By hanging around with the two of them so much, I got to learn a whole lot about Jewish culture. I went to their kids' bar mitzvahs and sat shiva with them when they lost a loved one. I came to respect and admire them through the ways they cared for their families and celebrated their traditions—and, for their part, they learned how things were with me and my boys and got to know *our* families and traditions.

We learned from each other, drew inspiration from each other.

This had a direct benefit to our working partnership, because Bruce and Norman were the first to admit they didn't know a thing about hip-hop. (You can bet they weren't reaching for NWA when it came time to karaoke—they'd lean as far as the Commodores or Stevie Wonder, but that was about it.) And we didn't know a thing about manufacturing on a mass scale, so we had these complementary skill sets and backgrounds. That's how it should be in any partnership, I came to realize. After all, if they knew everything *I* knew, there'd be no room in our deal for me. On the flip side, if I knew everything they did about manufacturing and distribution, there'd be no reason for me to work with *them.*

Matter of fact, that's one of the things I listen for when I'm hearing a *Shark Tank* pitch on the set. I want to know if an entrepreneur is simply out looking for financing or the publicity that comes from being on the show, or if there's really some way for me to attach my particular skill sets to their particular needs. At the same time, I want to know I'm dealing with an entrepreneur who recognizes their limitations. If they're all about going it alone and doing their own thing, it's probably not the deal for me— even if it's a tremendous product or concept. With me, it should be all about fit—so like it was with Bruce and Norman early on, I'm out to work with partners who want to lift each other up instead of pushing others aside.

No question about it, FUBU would never have grown so fast, so *hard,* if we didn't have all these component parts working in sync—because, hey, it's always better to ride together than to fly solo.

BE A WORTHWHILE INVESTMENT

Connections aren't limited to people. You'll want to find ways to connect to your target market, and to the industry you're looking to fit yourself into. **Here it pays to be hyper-specific about what you're hoping to achieve, and what your customers or your audience appear to value.** Best way to do this is to keep your eyes open for others who've been down this road before, and to cultivate relationships with people in a position to help you build the influence you'll need.

Then you want to prove to them that you're worth investing in—emotionally, financially, whatever. This was made clear to me the moment we had some powerful backers behind us—and with them, a little bit of momentum. At first, I closed my eyes and saw all those dollar signs and assumed there'd be tons of money for advertising and promotion, but that's not really how it happened. The financing we needed was to help us fill all the orders we wrote at our very first trade show, so even with deep pockets behind us, it still fell to us to push our clothes the same way we'd always pushed our clothes. The grind never stops—even when you're blessed to have some support behind you. In fact, you could make the argument that **the moment you get some support behind you is the moment you have to start grinding even harder, because there's more at stake.** People are investing in you, and you feel all this pressure to make sure they get a return on that investment.

So I got with Keith, Carl, and J and we took it up a couple notches, doing what we'd always done, this time with the confidence that comes from knowing our ask had some credibility behind it. Having a big backer in the fashion industry made us legit, in a meaningful way. There was a little extra juice to our mojo, and what that meant was that there was a kind of *powershift* on the back of our new status. Don't get me wrong: We were still out there chasing the same deals, hustling to make every sale, but now the deals came with a little less sweat and effort, now that we were playing at this new level.

THE POWER OF 6X

One of the things we noticed early on at FUBU was that every time we sold an item to a big customer—I'm talking size triple X, 4X, 5X, even 6X—he'd usually wear it into the ground. Just so happens that in the African American community, there are a lot of big, big guys—like, *really* big. And here it also happened that clothing manufacturers weren't making a whole lot of inventory for that particular demographic—like, hardly any at all.

We were the same way, at first, but then I saw an opportunity. Nothing against any of the big guys I knew, but I was still thinking in billboard terms. I mean, there was a *ton* of free advertising real estate available on a 6X guy's back, and most of them tended to work as bouncers, bodyguards, or security at the popular clubs all over the city, so they were pretty high-profile. What we had already learned by this point was that **giveaways and promo items play a big part in creating buzz in the fashion industry.** You toss around a little free merch to get noticed . . . that's just how it goes. Only, the big guys who worked as muscle in and around the club scene, the guys who worked as part of the crew on all these music video sets, they tended to get overlooked by companies like ours, so my thinking was we should start showing them a little love.

The skinny, cool people, they'd wear your stuff once or

twice and then your product would slide to the back of the closet and never see the light of day—or they'd give those shirts away or toss 'em because they were getting a ton of free stuff. You have to realize, I needed these big bouncer-types in my corner. They were gatekeepers, right? I needed them to wave me into the clubs or onto the set, to slip me the intel on who was inside, who was coming, who was going. But I couldn't give these guys shirts that were three or four sizes too small, so I made up a bunch of these 6X shirts and started spreading them around. It ended up, we got a lot of bang for the buck with those shirts, because these guys really appreciated the attention.

Most designers were tossing free product to the artists, and to the people who usually worked the front of the house at these venues. That's just how it went. So we kind of turned that whole transaction upside down, and these big and tall guys really appreciated it, and the effort returned some great dividends for us. Plus, like I said, there was a whole lot of room across those barrel chests and big bellies, so our FB logos and our FUBU logos were *really* on display.

One particular story stands out. I gave a shirt to a guy named Beast, who was head of security for Ralph McDaniels, one of the most influential figures on New York's hip-hop scene. Ralph was a producer and director, but he also hosted his own show called *Video Music Box* that was on WNYC-TV, a local public television station, and still exists today. Everybody I knew stopped what they were doing to watch that show. Everybody *I wanted to sell to* stopped what they were doing to watch that show. Every hip-hop artist wanted to be *on* that show, so it was pretty much required viewing in our little corner of the world. Talk about a billboard! Ralph's show could make or break a career, so of course it had me thinking it could make or break our clothing line as well. That's why it paid to get in good with Beast, and some of the other guys Ralph had working security—and here it worked out that Beast introduced us to Ralph directly and from that we were able to get on the *Video Music Box* set to flash some of our styles.

But here's the thing: It's not like we went up to these guys and said, *Hey, here is a 6X shirt we've made just for you because you're a really big guy and in exchange for our consideration we would really like it if you could help us out.* No, the reason our little promo outreach was effective was because it was *sincere.* We wanted Beast and them to know we had their backs, so we slapped a couple shirts on those backs and tried to take care of them. We were doing them a solid, and when we needed *them* to do a solid for *us,* we weren't coming at them cold.

What can I say? We were all about the little guy at FUBU, even if the "little guy" in this case weighed over three hundred pounds.

When you're developing your reputation, **there needs to be an equal give-and-take.** That's why we made it a point to get along with everybody, in every aspect of the music business, the media business, the fashion business: because you never know when you'll need a favor.

This give-and-take applies not just to individuals but to

communities, too. Relatively early on in the FUBU days—
before we'd even scored our first investor—it felt like we'd
done everything we could to get things going in our own
neighborhood. So we set our sights on the biggest trade
show in the fashion business. Everybody told us we should
be hitting the trade shows, so to us that meant we should
go big. Plus, you know, it made sense: In order to grow our
little upstart brand, we needed to put ourselves where the
business was—and where the business was, just then, was
Las Vegas.

Probably, we were getting a little ahead of ourselves.
Probably, we could have found opportunities for growth a
little closer to home. Even before being connected with
Samsung, we didn't have the money to get to Vegas for our
very first MAGIC show—the name stood for "Men's Apparel Guild in California," but by the time we hit the scene
everyone was just calling it by its acronym. Luckily, we
scored a bunch of companion tickets from my mother's
airline job and took turns flying standby until we were
able to make it to the convention floor. (It took a couple
days for some of us, thanks to some dicey connections, but
we all made it out there eventually!) And then we realized
we didn't have the money to take a booth at the show, so
we skimped and scraped until we scored a couple floor
tickets that allowed us to walk the aisles of that convention
like we belonged, trying to turn some heads and create
some buzz.

Our "showroom" for the run of the show was a hotel
room about five miles from the convention center. It wasn't

a suite or anything—just a basic one-bedroom, barely enough room for a couple racks to showcase our clothes. One of us slept in the bathtub; two of us slept on the floor; and two of us shared the bed, head-to-toe. When buyers on the floor responded to our pitch in a positive way, we'd find a way to drag them back to our room to check out our full line, hoping like crazy nobody could tell there were five of us staying in that one small room and that we were only playing at being big designers.

When we got back to New York (separately, since we'd had to split up at the Vegas airport and grab whatever standby connecting flights we could find), we huddled up and decided that for the time being at least, we were better off keeping our efforts close to home. Then we got the idea to create a billboard campaign to promote the brand in our own backyard. Problem was, there was no money for a traditional billboard campaign, so we went looking for urban display spaces we could hit up on the cheap. **The thinking here was,** *Hey, we'll create our own damn billboards.*

Turned out, we didn't have to look far. Do you know those pull-down security gates you see at mom-and-pop stores throughout the city? They're like rolling steel garage doors, except they usually look like graffiti-stained eyesores. Well, we went around talking to dozens of boutique clothing store owners and offered to clean up their security gates, provided that when we were done we could spray-paint some colorful artwork on them. The gates said "authorized FUBU dealer." The "makeovers" cost a couple of spray cans per gate, and for that we got about eight to ten hours of late-night display advertising at each spot, in neighborhoods all across the city. And do you want to know something? Those gates looked sharp ... especially when you compared them with how they'd looked before.

This guerrilla billboard campaign made a big impression. Whenever those gates were down, there was the FUBU name for all to see, and it would be on display all the way through to the morning rush hour in most spots. We got such a great response, we eventually started chasing the same setup in some neighborhoods in Philadelphia as well.

End of the day, we learned a powerful lesson: Even when it feels to everyone else like you should be playing in a bigger arena, on a bigger stage, that's when you should be doubling down on the people and communities that got you your shot in the first place.

Again, this isn't a strategy I'd studied in a book. Wasn't something I learned in some business or marketing class. It's just common sense: If you want good things to happen for you, you've got to be generous with what you put out into the community. That's how you build the foundation you'll need to stand upon when you *powershift* into the future.

KEEP WINNING AND YOU'LL GET EVERYONE'S ATTENTION

For an inspiring example of someone who's spent a lifetime making these points of connection in service of her goals, I want to introduce you to Billie Jean King. Everybody's heard of Billie, right? They've even named a whole tennis complex after her—the Billie Jean King National Tennis Center, home of the US Open. That's like *officially* changing the name of Yankee Stadium to "The House That Ruth Built" to honor the role Babe Ruth played in helping to establish the Yankees as a dominant force, which gets close to the impact Billie has had on her sport.

I have the honor of working with Billie through the United States Tennis Association Foundation, where we both sit on the Celebrity and Player Advisory Council, and I've come to admire her tenacity and her commitment to not only *doing* the right thing but also surrounding herself with people in a position to help her get that right thing done. Knowing how dedicated she is to supporting the USTA Foundation's goals of bringing education and tennis to underresourced communities, I could only imagine what she was like during her heyday fighting for equal rights.

What first struck me about Billie when we met and got to talking was that she thinks of herself as a small business owner and not as a former athlete. Think about that for a moment. And, she says, she's *always* thought of herself in this way. Think about that, too. Now, if you know the story of Billie's career, this might seem like a remarkable take— but then when you break it down, it seems to tie in perfectly with the way she's lived her life away from the tennis court, fighting battle after battle to bring about big change. She's got this scrappy, start-up mentality that leaves her looking at every issue like it matters most of all.

If you *don't* know the story of Billie's career, let me fill you in. For a long time—in the mid '60s to early '70s—she was the most dominant female tennis player in the world. You could make the case that she was the most dominant athlete, male or female, in any sport. Her twenty career titles at Wimbledon (six in singles, ten in doubles, four in mixed doubles) are still the most all-time.

But it's what she did with her all-time greatness that earns Billie a place in this conversation, and I write this as someone who didn't know a whole lot about tennis history before I met Billie. I didn't know how players had to struggle back in the day just to make a living—women, especially. Billie was determined to change all of that. Even when she was winning major tournaments and being talked about as one of the best players in the world, she couldn't afford to give up her gig as a playground instructor in Los Angeles, so it was a different game back then. Today you can be ranked in the triple digits and find a way to attract sponsors and pocket enough prize money at some under-the-radar tournaments to somehow make a living. That wasn't the case in Billie's day, and the reasons it up and changed have a whole lot to do with her. It was Billie who led the way to establishing the first professional women's tennis tour, before she went out and became the first president of the Women's Tennis Association and one of the founders of World Team Tennis.

And it was Billie who stood up to Bobby Riggs in the famous "Battle of the Sexes," beating the former champion in straight sets at the Houston Astrodome on September 20,

1973, in front of a worldwide television audience. When she decided to face off with this retired pro who couldn't stop talking about how female tennis players were inferior to their male counterparts, she did so knowing that it wasn't enough to simply stand across the net from this guy and give it her best: She had to win. She knew the exhibition match would offer her a once-in-a-lifetime platform, a chance to lobby for equal pay for women in tennis and to score a monumental victory for women's rights, so she wasn't just playing for her own personal bragging rights. She was representing a movement, fighting on behalf of women all over the world, and she refused to let them down.

From the very beginning, Billie was fighting for gender equality in tennis, and in sports in general. She was fighting for equal pay, equal opportunity, equal everything. Basically, she was a tennis champion on the court—and off the court a champion for social justice. And she knew, even from the moment she first picked up a racket as a little girl, that tennis could give her the platform to help bring about meaningful change, not just in her sport but in the world beyond tennis.

BILLIE JEAN KING, on making an impact: "Everyone talks about getting a seat at the table. I go, 'No, no, no, it's not a seat at the table. It's a voice at the table.'"

One of the great things about Billie is that when she sets her mind to something, she's all over it. The second time she picked up a racket, she says, she knew what she wanted to do with her life. "I raced home to tell my mother," she remembers. "I said, 'Mom, I know what I want to be. I want to be the number one tennis player in the world.' My mother could not believe it. She's going, 'That's fine, honey. You've got homework.' I said, 'No, Mom. You don't understand. This is what I want, I'm telling you.' And then, jump ahead to when my mother was eighty years old. I caught her looking at me one day and I said, 'Mom, what are you looking at?' And she goes, 'I remember that day when you got in the car and told me you wanted to be number one in the world.' But that's the life I wanted for myself. That's the life I wanted to make happen."

Pretty amazing, huh? Here I think it helps to know that Billie originally wanted to play competitive softball and only switched to tennis after her parents convinced her it was a more appropriate sport for a young lady. Sports were a big deal in Billie's house when she was growing up. Her mother was a swimmer. Her father was a basketball player. Her younger brother played Major League Baseball for twelve seasons. To this day, Billie prefers team sports to individual sports—she says it pushes you to work with others, to collaborate, to learn to motivate yourself and your teammates to accomplish bigger things than you could ever hope to achieve on your own.

What's also amazing is the way Billie found she had more and more influence as a player as she moved up in the ranks. Almost as soon as she started playing competitively, her motivation became something more than just being the number one player in the world. It was more about getting what she deserved—not just for herself but for every woman on the circuit. People started to listen to her, more and more, and what she had to say was able to resonate, more and more, because of the lights-out way she played the game. As long as she kept winning, she had everybody's attention.

At one point, we got to talking about how to make the right impression when you're trying to call attention to a movement or a cause, and Billie gave me a great piece of advice. Actually, she gave me *three* pieces of advice, all rolled into one. She told me that when you're advocating for change, or looking to go against the grain on an issue, there are three things to keep in mind, together with Billie's takeaway on each:

1. Relationships are everything.

"This is the fundamental lesson of my life. The connections we make with others are so important."

2. Keep learning.

"And on top of that you've got to keep learning *how* to learn. We learn different things in different ways. So we have to be prepared to adapt."

3. Be a problem solver.

"When people start to realize that you're not just complaining about something, but that you've taken the time to come up with a solution, that's when you can be really effective."

"The one thing I always tell young players is to learn the business," Billie says. "It's basic. Learn about sponsorship partnerships. Learn the history. Learn what it means to have your own skin in the game."

What Billie discovered early on was that she had a way of connecting with people. She's one of the best there is at networking—at leveraging her many points of connection so that she can connect all those dots and create a kind of through-line to shift power from where she is to where she wants to go. For example, she got along with the reporters who covered the sport. She got that they were the ones who'd be telling her story, so she made sure they *understood* her story. She didn't do this in any kind of scheming or manipulative way. She'd simply built this reputation as someone who spoke her mind and stood up for what she thought was right, and people were drawn to that kind of empowering message. Plus, these people were all her friends, so they spent a lot of time with one another, got to know one another, looked for ways to support one another. That's how it goes sometimes when you're building a community in service of a shared goal.

She also found ways to connect with the sponsors she was hitting up to back the women's tour—again, not in a manipulative way but in a genuine, shared-mission sort of way. She was able to see the synergy in getting a company like Virginia Slims to sign on as a major tour sponsor, and to get excited about it in a way that also excited the executives who had to write the checks.

Just how are you supposed to develop the points of connection in your own life and career? Well, I've got some ideas . . . (and a special place for you to start implementing these in the workbook at DaymondJohn.com/Powershift Extras).

1. Develop name recognition.

Reinforcement is a powerful tool. Find a way to use whatever resources you have available to you to get and keep your name out there. Tell a story about yourself, and make it memorable. Do your homework, and make sure the story you tell about yourself jibes with the stories that *others are telling about you.*

2. Learn to open a new file every time you make a new relationship.

Somebody gave me the idea not too long ago when I myself was struggling with this to create a kind of file in my head for every contact in my address book, and it's been enormously helpful in keeping my connections straight. Think of it like creating a new file folder on your computer every time you work on a specific task for a specific project. I don't even have to write everything down—just thinking about it in this way helps me to organize my thoughts. I come up with a header and everything, then file the exchange in a way I'll be able to call back to mind.

Specifically, the person who shared this approach

with me pointed out that someone we knew had this habit of doing a cartoonish double take whenever you went to him with an idea, almost like Scooby-Doo, so now whenever I think of that person he's filed away in my head under Scooby-Doo. It's become a great memory prompt for me. Now if I see someone once a year and we always go out for sushi, that's how I call that person to mind—it's become our point of connection. If someone's in the habit of sending me a thoughtful gift or a handwritten note, that's how I tend to remember that person. If we met on the beach at a resort we were both staying at for a conference, that mental file will be filled with sand.

3. Think through the immediate obstacles you can expect to find in your path.

If you know what to expect, you know what's expected, so lay out all the pitfalls and roadblocks and figure out in advance how you mean to get around them.

4. Understand your target audience, and let that understanding drive your decision making.

In business, the customer is always right. In building your personal brand, the same thinking applies—only here the focus should be on honoring the target audience for your idea ... and finding ways to double down and deliver on that idea.

5. Seek common ground.

In negotiating circles, there's an old rule of thumb that says if you're still looking for common ground when you sit down with someone at the negotiating table, you're already behind. The time to start forging these helpful relationships is *before* you need to call on someone for an assist.

POWER FACT Get out of your comfort zone. You can't sit back and expect opportunities to find you—you've got to put yourself out there and bring your product, your service, your pitch, your talents to wherever it is your audience gathers, whether conferences and trade shows, on Twitter and Instagram, online, or elsewhere.

Chapter 6

REFINE YOUR APPROACH

No matter how much you prepare or how carefully you study the market, you just never know how things will go until you're out in the arena, so one of the things I tell aspiring entrepreneurs is to be constantly aware of what they're putting out into the world. This is especially true today, in our digital age, when even the slightest misstep or miscalculation can follow you around forever, like a piece of toilet paper stuck to your shoe.

Making the right kind of impression isn't *just* about avoiding potential embarrassment, however. It's also about reading the room and evaluating the market in a way that allows you to reposition yourself or your business if things aren't working out. Throughout these pages, we've looked at ways we might pivot into an exciting new opportunity—to *powershift* from a position of strength into a whole new position of strength. But before we can find those opportunities, we must sometimes pivot onto an entirely new approach, rethink our strategy, and even modify our goals. So what I also tell entrepreneurs is that they should always have a backup plan.

Setting a course of action doesn't mean you won't need to make a course correction—that's why I'm a big believer in having a fallback option. A lot of people don't agree with me on this, I should mention. There's a theory in some business circles that in order to truly succeed you need to "burn the boats." That's a leadership strategy that reaches all the way back to the sixteenth century, when the Spanish conquistador Hernán Cortés led an armada of eleven boats and six hundred men on an expedition to Mexico. When he got there, he ordered his men to destroy his ships, letting them know they had no choice but to fight and win. Retreating was no longer an option.

I've always admired the back-against-the-wall spirit of that lesson, but in my own life I like to have options. I like to know that if I can't win the battle, I can live to fight another day. After all, it's how we regroup after a disappointment or a false start that can sometimes make the biggest difference in the end.

On the professional front, you always want to move ahead with a sound business plan, but underneath or alongside you want to give yourself some options. You know—take some affordable next steps. As individuals, we should also have fallback strategies for when the message we mean to send doesn't hit its mark. In order to maximize your results and achieve your goals, you must be brave enough to step back, examine your successes and failures, and go back to the drawing board.

Problem is, a lot of times, if you don't go back to the drawing board until you're up against it, you're too late. The idea, really, is to think through a bunch of different scenarios before you set out to establish yourself or launch a new product or business. Think about some of the block-buster companies that for some reason weren't able to pivot or transition to changes in technology or public behavior—like, say, Blockbuster Video, where executives allegedly passed on an opportunity to partner in some way with an online DVD rental outlet called Netflix. Or BlackBerry, Myspace, Kodak, or any other company that somehow went from dominance to irrelevance because they failed to look ahead at what was coming. That's why you need to go about your business with your head up, and be prepared to face a roadblock or a hiccup or two, so it pays to spend some time to think about what can be wrong for you or your business. They don't all have to be worst-case scenarios, but they should be less than ideal.

What happens if you expected to be first to market with a product or service and by the time you're up and running you spot a viable competitor in the field?

How do you reposition yourself as a kind of tastemaker if you're consistently slow to spot the latest trend or style?

What do you do when you find success and then you start to see things you can be doing better or more efficiently?

How do you respond when your year-over-year growth is beyond what you'd ever imagined but is still trailing the growth of your competitors?

If you address these scenarios *before* you head back to the drawing board, you'll at least have something on that board to consider. Sometimes this can result in a sharp pivot. Sometimes it's simply about fine-tuning and recommitting to your initial objective. Either way, this is a necessary part of building lasting and sustainable influence, and you'll want to be prepared to respond quickly to any changes in the marketplace, in public opinion, or in the ways you or your brand are being perceived.

KNOW WHEN TO MAKE YOUR MOVE

Billy Gene Shaw is one of smartest digital marketers on the planet. I met Billy when I was trying to generate some buzz for "Daymond on Demand," the online curriculum I offer for entrepreneurs and corporations looking to tap into some of the ideas and principles I discuss in my books and in my speeches and educational workshops. I was always on the lookout for talented digital marketers who really seemed to understand Facebook ads and other online platforms, and I was enormously impressed by Billy's instinct for this type of marketing.

Billy gets that the real power of Facebook ads is the way they allow you to change things up on the fly, without having to throw a ton of money at a campaign. Instead of making a major media buy for tens of thousands of dollars, you can get the word out on Facebook for a couple hundred bucks—and then, when you see how customers are responding to it (or *not* responding to it, as the case may be), you can make some changes and go at it another way.

The thing about Billy, as I came to know once we got friendly, was that he lived his life in much the same way. He tried things one way for a while, and if whatever he was doing wasn't working he tried it another way. And so on. For a while in there, Billy was kind of treading water, unable to get any kind of career going. He'd gone to college because his parents taught him that he would be the first in the family to get an education. This was a big deal, because both of his parents had grown up on welfare. On almost every limb of his family tree there was a sad story of drug addiction, gambling, or gang violence.

As a young African American male growing up in San Diego, Billy felt like he only had two good options in life. Oh, there were plenty of *bad* options all around, but if he wanted to lift himself up and out it felt to him like he could chase a career in either music or sports ... and that was about it. Those were the easy money plays. Trouble was, he didn't really have the chops for either, so he stuck to school. His father had gotten it together to make a decent living selling cars, so it just worked out that the thing Billy decided to study was business, even though he didn't really have any background or familiarity with the business world. In his mind, studying business was a path toward learning how to make money, but no one in his family had run a business, and as far as he knew he'd never even met an entrepreneur. He didn't even know what the stock market was. When one of his professors asked for a show of hands in class one day to see how many students had money invested in the market, Billy had no idea what the guy was talking about.

"I was so intimidated," he says now of that moment in the classroom when he was found out in this way. "I was like, I'm outta here. I don't need this crap."

Billy was in his junior year by this point, and he was carrying all this pressure to do well in school and to make something of himself, but he was going down a road with no map, no frame of reference for what it would take to succeed. Maybe that's why when an invitation came from his girlfriend's family to join them on a vacation to Cabo, he was all over it even though he still had one class to finish before graduation, and when he went to the professor to make some kind of arrangement to complete the work he'd miss, she pushed back. It was early in the semester, and Billy thought the professor would cut him some slack since he was giving her a ton of notice and offering to make up the work on a different schedule, but she told him she wouldn't let him pass the course if he missed the final few sessions and wasn't able to sit for the final, so Billy got his back up.

"I went to Cabo anyway," he told me, "because I hated

the feeling that this professor controlled me. She had this power over me that was going to dictate whether I was going to succeed in life or fail, and I just found it so insulting and frustrating. I was like, 'I don't need your approval. I don't need a piece of paper telling me I passed this one course. I don't even need my degree.' It wasn't the smartest decision in the world, but I was dug in, and just like she said, I didn't pass her class. I didn't graduate. And my parents didn't really talk to me for two years."

Billy was determined to move forward on his terms and his terms alone. But as he soon learned, when you get it in your head that you can seize the power in a situation by doing whatever you damn well please, without first putting in the work, you set yourself up to fail.

That's a hard lesson to take in at any age, but it's especially tough when you're young and just starting out—and even harder when you feel like you're carrying your family's hopes and dreams. So here Billy had left himself no choice but to refine his approach and come at life in a whole other way. "I was doing the entrepreneur thing because I wanted to but I also had to," Billy says. "I had to win. Like, if I didn't win, that was it."

Now, Billy's gone on to have some serious success in digital marketing, so I feel comfortable giving him some grief over this, but I'm sharing the story of Billy's *powershift* fail because it reminds us that we can't snap our fingers and expect to gain the upper hand in each and every transaction or negotiation. That's not the way it works. Remember, the foundation of this *powershift* principle is that you have to first *build a foundation*—something Billy seemed to miss in this case. He had no power in this situation, no standing—and it cost him.

The better play, the *only* play, is to set things up so that when you *do* need someone else's permission or blessing, they have no choice but to grant it. But you've got to *earn* these things, not just *ask* for them.

Underneath all of that, however, is a deeper truth that Billy also acknowledges: He had a limiting set of beliefs that basically served to stiff-arm him from his goals. Because of the hardscrabble way he grew up, he was conditioned to think there was a kind of ceiling to what he could accomplish, and when he started bumping up against that ceiling he couldn't find a way to power through.

At least, not at first. It took him a couple stops and starts. It took moving back into his parents' house and finding a way to get them to forgive him for sabotaging his college degree the way he did. And it took a failed attempt at a mobile oil-changing business that seemed like a good idea at the time. But he kept at it, until he finally stumbled on something that he was uniquely good at. He said to himself, "I didn't have the paper and I wasn't the smartest dude. What can I do that everyone can't?" Turned out that Billy's strength—the thing he could do better than just about everyone else—was in helping people grow their online businesses, which in turn became *his* online business.

BILLY GENE SHAW, on learning to get out of his own way: "I was twenty-three, I didn't graduate from college,

I cursed like a sailor. But there I was trying to reach my target demographic, who was probably a forty-five-year-old white guy who was married and absolutely did go to college and probably even had a master's degree. So my mind game around that was really twisted, but then I learned something. People only care about one color in business. Green. Period. If I can make these guys money, it doesn't matter if I have a degree, or if I'm black. A lot of that was just in my head."

One of the first businesses Billy knew he could help was a local Orangetheory Fitness center. Today Orangetheory is one of the leading on-site fitness franchises in the world, with over one thousand locations in over twenty countries. But back then, it was just a string of US franchisees struggling to build a *brand* . . . and a *lifestyle*.

So Billy hit up one of their locations and offered his services and got hired to do a one-shot campaign. But then just as his marketing plan was about to go live online, he got a call from the manager, who was having second thoughts on moving forward. Obviously, Billy was far from thrilled. By this point, he'd already spent a couple days building the campaign, and he knew it would work, and now here this guy was telling him they'd just hired someone from Equinox who was claiming that Facebook ads don't work. Billy was at the stage where every lead mattered, every dollar counted, and he wasn't about to let this opportunity slip, so he offered to pay back his fee—

three times over—if his push didn't connect with customers. He set it up so the manager had nothing to lose, so he couldn't say no. So of course the guy grabbed at these new terms—and sure enough, the moment Billy's campaign went live the inquiries came pouring in. In fact, he generated *123 leads* for that one Orangetheory location in the very first day—more than they typically pulled in a month!—and out of that success he went on to build similar campaigns for more than 300 Orangetheory gyms.

No, he still didn't have that college diploma, but he'd discovered something even better. He had a skill, a talent: He really understood this online advertising thing—back at a time when few other people did.

Once Billy figured this out, it's like he was lit from within. All of a sudden, he was able to put himself out there with confidence and certainty, knowing that he had real value to offer his potential clients. He didn't have his hand out, the way he did with that professor who wouldn't cut him any slack. Instead he was coming from a place of strength, offering to small firms online advertising strategies that he was dead solid certain would transform their businesses.

Today Billy Gene Shaw is one of the most respected video and strategic advertising experts in the field. He's the master of running online traffic, and he's lately expanded his efforts to teach what he's learned in a series of wildly popular online courses. His thing is helping brands turn clicks into customers, and if you ask me, he's the best in the business. (And I would know, because he continues to help me drive traffic to my own online workshops and products.) More important, his story shows us the power to be found when you make your move from a place of authority—on your own time, in your own way.

What are some of the ways you can set yourself up to move with the same kind of authority in your own life and career?

1. Don't be afraid to start small.

When you're out to establish a reputation, you don't want to take on anything more than you can handle. That's why Billy started off with just that onetime campaign for Orangetheory Fitness. He understood that the key to establishing credibility is to demonstrate your ability to deliver. So be sure you're not biting off more than you can chew and that you're only making promises you can keep.

2. Understand that as you are out there trying to tell your own story, others are looking for ways to translate what you're doing to their stories.

We're not the only ones trying to build influence and make our special brand of noise. The people we're looking to sell to, or impress, or otherwise win over to whatever it is we're trying to do, all have their own agendas working as well, so look for ways to get both sets of goals in alignment.

3. Don't get discouraged.

This one's easier said than done, of course, but keep your chin up. Keep at it. And know that it takes time to make a lasting impression.

POWER FACT According to a study published in the *Journal of Business Venturing*, a shorter and less detailed business plan is often better than a larger, very specific one because it allows you to be more nimble and refine your strategies and approaches more easily. The researchers found that having a business plan is important, but its value is more in allowing businesses to clearly see and adjust their strategies than as a road map for the future of the company.

PART II

NEGOTIATE
Make a Deal

The second gear you'll need to hit when you're looking to shift power and take control of any situation is to master your negotiating skills. It's one thing to establish your credibility and reputation in such a way that others will want to deal with you; it's another thing entirely to be able to close that deal. Figure out what you want to make happen, and then learn to read the room in ways that serve you and bring you closer to your goals.

Chapter 7

DO YOUR HOMEWORK

Think back to when you were in school: You didn't sit for an exam without reading the material, studying your notes, and trying to figure out what might be on the test.

Think back to day one on the job: You didn't just show up without first learning about the company, about the office culture, about your competition.

Think back to that time your partner brought you home to meet his or her parents: You didn't show up before pumping your partner with questions, getting the lay of the land, understanding the family history, maybe some of the family dynamic.

Point is, if you don't do your homework, chances are you won't find success.

The same deal applies when you start in on a negotiation . . . *any* negotiation . . . *every* negotiation. Doesn't matter what's being discussed. Doesn't matter who the other players are, or what's at stake. What matters is that you do some prep before you come to the table, that you have a clear idea what you hope to get out of the deal . . . and why you deserve it.

We've already talked about how some of that prep is about making the right kind of noise and laying your foundation. But before you roll up your sleeves and have at it, you also have to **take the time to understand the situation for what it is.** Make an honest assessment. Look around and see how you've fit yourself into this picture. Know that you are not here for some random reason. You didn't win a lottery that put you in this position. Nobody picked your name out of a hat and called you in for an interview. No, you're here because you've earned yourself a place at this table, because you have something real and tangible to offer. Maybe it's your money, or your legit expertise and insights, or a complementary skill set. Maybe your rep alone is worth something to the deal going forward.

Looking back, I can see that in every deal I've ever done, every transaction I've tried to make happen, I needed to know there was power on my side of the table. Like I wrote earlier, this wasn't something I studied or worked toward. It was just something I knew in my gut. Deep down, I knew I needed to be the disruptive force in the room, to *be* the change I wanted to make happen, so I found a way to step into that role. I made sure there was nobody else on the planet who could deliver on a deal the way I could deliver on a deal—and the reason I was able to do *that* with dead solid certainty was because of all the ways I'd carried myself until just that moment.

All that noise we talked about making in Part I of the book? This is where you start to put it all in play.

Look around your town, your city, wherever you happen to live. Check out the historic buildings that make up your skyline. Those iconic buildings that have been around forever are iconic for a reason, right? They've been built on a solid foundation, so there's a good chance they'll be around forevermore. That's kind of what we're shooting for here when I talk about making noise and building influence and seeding your future with a solid foundation. That skyline has been built to last . . . and so have you. **In every negotiation, your reputation precedes you.** You don't want to be that guy who asks for the moon and stars and then has to explain why you're worth the moon and stars—it should be obvious to everyone in that room. They should be gift-wrapping the moon and stars for you before you even sit down.

One of the things you have to realize, young people especially, is that *everything* you do, *everything* you say, and *everything* you put out into the world contributes in some way to your reputation. We've all got a kind of "social thumbprint," a permanent record of the way we live our lives in this electronic age, and you don't want to be caught thinking that what you share online is just something for you and your friends. I know that when I'm interviewing a candidate for a job, or meeting someone to talk about a deal, I'll check out their social media before we get together, just to see what I can see. It's not snooping—it's due diligence. If there's information out there that can help me form a first impression about someone, I'm gonna grab at it. And you can be sure that when you're up for a job or out to do a deal, the person on the other side of the table will be doing the same thing when it comes to you.

I don't say this as a way to get you to try to live off the grid, though, since a recent CareerBuilder survey found that nearly half of employers (47 percent!) see having no online footprint as a red flag. So take advantage of the opportunity that social media provides for you to portray your best features online; just keep in mind who might be looking at your pages.

Your rep is your skyline. People should be able to see it from miles and miles away. They should know what it stands for, what you put into it . . . what they can expect from you as you move forward. But if you want to be the disruptive force in this transaction, you first have to see yourself as others see you—and see where you fit as you stand alongside everyone else.

Everything else flows from this right here.

DO YOUR HOMEWORK

UNDERSTAND THE LANDSCAPE

My role on *Shark Tank* gives me a front-row seat to the many ways aspiring entrepreneurs and innovators pitch their businesses and products. Some of them prepare for the big day by learning everything there is to know about their market and their competitors, memorizing every dollar amount or data point relevant to their financial picture, and trying to anticipate every question we might throw at them. Others take a more seat-of-the-pants approach and figure they can just wing it once the cameras are rolling. Most fall somewhere in between.

Still, even after eleven seasons, those people who walk in there without a well-thought-out pitch always catch me by surprise. It happens all the time, and when it does I scratch my head and wonder how lazy or stupid or full of yourself you have to be to get this amazing opportunity to pitch your business or product on *Shark Tank* and kick it to the curb in this way. It's like going for a job interview without even doing the most basic, Wikipedia-type research on a company. Something you might think everyone knows to do, right? Wrong. You'd be surprised to know that according to a CareerBuilder survey, only 64 percent of candidates actually research a company online after applying, and 67 percent of candidates will continue with their application even if they cannot find any information online about the company. You definitely don't want to be that candidate that shows up to an interview with no knowledge about the company, and that's exactly how the entrepreneurs who pitched to us on *Shark Tank* without doing their research on us appeared. We saw a lot more of these dud pitches early on, before the show became a kind of cultural marker and an obvious make-or-break opportunity for people lucky enough to make it onto our set. But even now we get our share of entrepreneurs who show up totally unprepared. It's gotten to the point where some of the viewers know what makes a good or bad pitch better than the person up there making it. I can picture people sitting at home watching and yelling at the television set like it's a horror movie—only instead of "don't go into the basement!" they're yelling "offer another 5 percent!"

People are always asking how to get on the show, or what they should do if they make it to the Tank. The first question, I'm not really able to answer—the producers have that one figured out. But the second question, I'm able to share what I look for in a pitch. It's tough to generalize, because every pitch is different, every prospect is different. Sometimes I'm listening for an opportunity in a field I already know something about, and sometimes I'm intrigued by a business that's entirely new to me. What usually happens, though, is that I'm looking at three main components in the pitch—and they all come down to how well (or how little!) the entrepreneur prepared for this moment.

Here are those components:

- The first thing I look for is **confidence**. When I see entrepreneurs who believe in themselves, or in their business or product, my ears perk up. Probably the worst mistake you can make on our set is to bring a take-it-or-leave-it attitude with you into the Tank. Believe me, if that's your style, the Sharks will *leave it*—and you'll be back where you started. At the same time, you don't want to be too, too full of yourself. There's a fine line between confidence and blowhardiness, so my advice to any entrepreneur— whether on *Shark Tank* or not—is to try not to come off as "all that and then some." Instead, know your stuff, *own* your stuff, and your belief in your business will shine through. And whatever you do, don't come at us with one of those lines like, "Hey, it's a $50 billion industry, so if we can capture just 1 percent of that market we're good to go." A line like that, it's a sure sign you haven't done your homework and that you're playing us Sharks for fools.

• Next, I look to the **valuation**. A lot of times, entrepreneurs will come on the show with an inflated idea of what their business is worth. Maybe they have no substantial sales to date, or maybe they haven't secured the necessary patents they need to protect their invention. You can usually tell right away when an ask is way out of line with what a company might be worth, and when I see that it gets my back up. I'm not interested in negotiating with someone from a place of unreason, and the way the show is set up I don't have to, so I'll just bow out at this point. Your valuation is important to us, because it helps us to see your situation as you see it, which may or may not line up with how things truly are. Plus, if your numbers aren't tight, it'll be that much harder for you to take in funding. In fact, that's the number one reason African American companies have a hard time getting financing—because they tend to treat their bottom line and their balance sheet as afterthoughts. When I hear a crazy valuation on *Shark Tank,* I assume one or more of the following to be true: (a) the business is bleeding cash left and right; (b) the person up there doesn't actually want a deal, they just want a commercial; or (c) the founders just don't value our time enough to be bothered to do some homework. As a general rule, when pitching your business, you should take the time to properly value it, in a way that's supported by your income, your assets, and your reasonable projections.

• Finally, I look to the **professionalism** of the pitch. I'm a sucker for props and pie charts and visual aids that help to signal where you are in the marketplace, or where you hope to be in the near future. And if you've got samples, be sure to bring them along. But take the time to make sure the packaging is just right, that the moving parts all move the way they're supposed to, and that any people who might be helping you with your demonstration are actually familiar with your product and how it's used. (Of course, those three explanations all take a back seat to the simple fact that sometimes the people doing the pitching must be lazy, careless, or flat-out unprepared.)

"Be prepared"—that's the Boy Scout motto, and it should be yours, too. Doesn't matter if you're making a pitch on *Shark Tank* or negotiating with your spouse over who gets to control the remote. You need to understand every aspect of that interaction before it takes place if you want things to lean your way.

I've been doing homework my entire life—maybe not for school, hunched over a textbook, but I've been studying just the same. I've studied the trends and studied the market in all the different areas and arenas I've played in. You can hardly blame me for expecting the entrepreneurs and business owners who walk into the Tank to do the same.

So you better believe I was impressed by Randy Goldberg and David Heath when they first showed up in the Tank. Randy and David are the founders of Bombas, the coolest sock makers on the planet. Their business is built on a give-back model that's helped to get them noticed—but even more than that, it's really helped to make the world a better place, because for every pair of socks they sell they donate another pair to a network of homeless shelters. How great is that? This one very basic charitable component set things up so that the story they get to tell about their business is not just about their socks but also about what each of us can do to help others in need.

I get asked all the time about my most successful partnerships to emerge from the show, and Bombas is right up there at the top of my list. They're also at the top of the list in terms of doing their homework, because these guys were so thoroughly and ridiculously prepared for whatever they might face in the Tank it's like nothing else mattered.

If you don't know the Bombas story, let me fill you in. Randy and David were born entrepreneurs—like, literally. David grew up packing samples in the basement for his father's business—making those wood chips you always see in parks and playgrounds, a pioneering safety initiative at the time. And Randy's parents ran an optical business, so he grew up going on trips with his father, selling frames and lenses to their accounts up and down the East Coast. So I think it's fair to say that starting their own business was in their DNA, and when David and Randy wound up working together at a lifestyle media company they got to talking and decided to get together on a joint venture. Trouble was, they couldn't figure out what kind of business they wanted to start. All they knew, really, was that they seemed to work well together and wanted to run their own show.

That all changed one day when David came across a Facebook post talking about how socks were the most requested item at homeless shelters nationwide—it was one of those *lightbulb over the head* moments. Right away, he got this idea to make and market a line of socks, and for every pair he sold he would donate a pair to the homeless community. To David, it was as much about the giving aspect of the transaction as it was about the socks, because up until this time he hadn't really given socks a whole lot of thought.

Randy was all over it as soon as David shared his idea, and from there they put a business plan in place that was as much about making money as it was about making a difference.

For these guys to make an impression on me was a big deal, because I have a warehouse full of FUBU socks. They're probably the toughest item of clothing to sell, because nobody really thinks much about them—they're like the underwear of the feet, right? For a lot of guys I know, they're an impulse buy; they just grab whatever's on sale at Filene's or Burlington Coat Factory.

Before Bombas, there was hardly any brand loyalty in this one segment of the apparel industry. But Bombas socks were different—or at least, they had the potential to be different. What these guys were selling, really, was a story, but they had the sense to know that in order for that story to resonate, they also had to make sure they were selling a first-rate product. Luckily, it turned out they knew just the person to help them with this. What happened was, early on in the development process, David was having dinner with his father and told him for the first time about his idea. His father pointed out that David's godfather had just retired from the sock business, and suggested that David and Randy tap this wealth of information and take some of the bumps out of the learning curve.

"We didn't know anything about sock manufacturing

or the apparel business," David recalls, "so this gave us a huge competitive advantage. We learned that if we wanted to make a dress sock, we should go here. For an athletic sock, we should go there. We learned about pricing. And these manufacturers took us much more seriously, because we had this great introduction, somebody to vouch for us. We weren't just a couple of kids who had no idea what they were doing."

Out of that great introduction, they were able to design what they believed was the perfect sock—one that didn't fall down or bunch up. (They even found a way to get rid of that annoying toe seam at the front!) At the same time, they designed a sock for the homeless population that featured an antimicrobial treatment and reinforced seams, knowing that these socks would probably get a whole lot more wear between washings.

It took about a year and a half before David and Randy believed they had a product they could share with the rest of the world, and as soon as they did they started selling direct to the consumer through their website. By the time they came to *Shark Tank* in the summer of 2014, about a year after launching their online business, they were seeking two hundred thousand dollars in funding for a 5 percent share in the company.

As a side note, I should mention here that Randy and David had it in their heads that a deal with me would be worth more to them than a deal with one of the other Sharks on the show. They studied the backgrounds and interests of everyone they were pitching and figured, all things being equal, they might as well target the guy in the fashion business as their future partner.

But that was just the beginning of their *Shark Tank* prep. Next thing they did before appearing was watch every episode. Yep, you read that right . . . *every single episode*. And they took notes! They treated it like a full-time job, compiling a list of every question ever asked by one of the Sharks. Alongside that, they put together another list of every conceivable question they thought they might be asked, and then they practiced their answers, even staging mock pitches with their friends. Randy told me later that their biggest fear was going on national television and being caught unprepared. "When you watch the show regularly, you see people going on there all the time and getting clowned by the Sharks," he says. "We didn't want that to happen."

They sure didn't. Which is why they were prepping for their pitch up until the very last minute. The week of their taping coincided with the 2014 World Cup, and they remember spreading out in the lobby of their hotel in LA, pretty much oblivious to the soccer game that was on in the background, while the rest of their Bombas team grilled them, going one by one through a monster list of questions.

DAVID HEATH, on what he and his partner took away from their extensive prep: "It forced us to examine every aspect of our business, and even if we'd gotten on the show and didn't make a deal or get a great mentor or supporter out of it, I think the exercise would have been super-useful for propelling us to the next level of our company. It set us up for what came next."

The great lesson here, for me, is that nothing good is lost when it comes to laying in a foundation for your pitch. **The work you put in will always pay you back— even if it takes a while before you start seeing those dividends.**

The Bombas pitch lasted over an hour, though you'd never know that from watching the edited version that eventually appeared on the show, which only ran about eight minutes. We really put these guys through the wringer, but they were prepared for everything we threw at them. They'd done their homework, that's for sure.

Hands down, my Bombas stake has turned out to be one of the best investments I've made on the show. Not only that, it's the #1 performing company in the history of *Shark Tank* in terms of sales—not bad for a couple of guys who were pretty new to the sock business when they came to our set. David and Randy set out to donate one million pairs of socks in their first ten years in business, but they got to that number in just two and a half. As I write this, they're hoping to cross the twenty-five-million threshold, and it fills my heart to know the good these guys are able to do on the back of every sale.

RANDY GOLDBERG, on giving back: "The driving force and the animus is this charitable connection to our community where we all work and live. That's been at the heart of Bombas from the very beginning. That mission, and our alignment around that mission, is the central factor in the work that everybody does in this company every day. It's a big part of our culture. Everybody knows why we're here, why this company was founded. You couldn't take that community element and remove it from Bombas, because we would cease to exist as a company."

PUT YOUR BEST FOOT FORWARD

When aspiring entrepreneurs ask me about what goes into a successful pitch on the show, I tell them that what gets me excited is what gets *them* excited. It might seem obvious, but I'm always going to be more drawn to entrepreneurs and business owners who are passionate about what they're making or selling or doing. By the same token, when I step back and look at the pitches I'm *least* excited about—even if it's a great product and the business looks great on paper—I realize the reason I'm not excited is because the people doing the pitching aren't all that excited.

The reality is, if it feels to me like you're just looking to make a buck, I'm probably going to tune you out. Why? Because then it's just about me betting on your product or concept. But if I sit across from you and really *feel* your obsession, your passion . . . if I get the sense that you eat, sleep, breathe, and *live* whatever it is you're making or selling . . . well, then I'm ready to listen, because then it's about me betting on *you.*

You better believe I felt that passion from Randy and David when they showed up to pitch Bombas. Sure, they're out to make money, and they're out to make the best damn sock in the business, but they're also out to make the world a better place, and this mission is what drives every decision they make. It's helped to position the company as a leader in its segment of the apparel industry. It's even helped them to negotiate better terms with their vendors, because people get excited about partnering with a company that contributes to the greater good. Also, we figured out that customers are inclined to reach for a pair of Bombas socks over another brand because they know their purchase will lead directly to the donation of a pair of socks to someone in need.

And yet the thing about the Bombas model is that it wasn't conceived as a strategy. David and Randy didn't build this charitable component into their business as a way to negotiate better terms or earn some positive PR. It might have played out that way, but this was never the objective. The charitable piece wasn't meant as a way to distinguish themselves from other brands—or to help them "get a leg up" on the competition. (You'll have to forgive me, but the dad pun was just too hard to resist!) No, it came from a genuine place—a genuine passion—that knocked my socks off (groan!) right off the bat.

Plus, it just so happens that purpose-driven companies like Bombas tend to have a lot of advantages baked in to their business plan. According to the Cone/Porter Novelli Purpose study, reported on the Engage for Good website, companies with a give-back component to their business are able to build stronger emotional ties with their customers than companies just out to make a buck. In the study, it said that two-thirds of consumers would be willing to switch brands if doing so meant they could turn a transactional purchase into a more meaningful one instead, along the lines of the Bombas give-back model.

COVER YOUR BASES . . . ALL OF YOUR BASES

Okay, we've covered the homework you need to do *before* you're even invited to the table—you know, to get you that invitation in the first place. (By the way, I should mention here that the Bombas team did so much homework in preparation for their *Shark Tank* pitch, they did my homework as well—meaning that I was able to learn so much more about sock manufacturing and distribution from them than I'd ever been able to pick up on my own.) But the work doesn't end there. Now you have to hit that meeting *hard,* and that means homework of a whole different kind—learning everything you can about your person (or persons) across the table, and making sure you have all the information you need at hand so that you're ready for any questions that might come your way. And when I say you need to learn *everything* you can about the people you're dealing with, I do mean everything—up to and including a person's tendencies or back story or outside interests so you can maybe refer back to them once the conversation gets going.

And remember that just because you know a person's past doesn't mean you know their present or their future. For example, if you did the bare minimum amount of homework, you'd know that I started my career in the clothing business, but you'd have to dig a lot deeper to learn that I'm a lot less excited about those kinds of opportunities at this current moment.

Keep in mind, negotiations are never as simple or clear-cut as we'd like them to be. They're loaded with all kinds of preconceptions and emotions, and to set yourself up to succeed you have to figure out what those are for the people sitting across the table from you. Are they coming at you with a nothing-to-lose mindset or an everything-to-gain attitude? Are they trying to get the better of you . . . or simply to get the best *out* of you? And are you absolutely sure that both sides are speaking the same language? A lot of times, what we hear as a yes is really meant as a *no,* so you have to be extra careful to make sure that you're understood and that you're clear on what you're getting back from the other side.

Just how are you supposed to learn all of this stuff? This part's easy, really. A quick Google search can reveal a whole lot of useful information. Go ahead and check out the people you're about to meet on Instagram or Twitter. You can learn a lot about someone by what they choose to share, and who they interact with online. You can also learn a lot from any friends or colleagues you have in common, so don't be shy about asking questions. Be honest about why you're asking—let your friends know that you're about to meet with this or that person and you were wondering if there's anything you should know about them.

We'll hit some of these strategies in more detail a little later on in these pages, but for now here are just a few things to keep in mind (with a corresponding section in the workbook at DaymondJohn.com/PowershiftExtras) as you get ready for any negotiation:

1. Identify the other person's motivation.

What's in it for them? The more you know about what the other person expects to get out of the deal, the more time you have to start thinking about what you're prepared to give.

2. Come prepared with questions.

For me, the most awkward part of a job interview is when I ask the person applying if they have any questions for me before we finish . . . and they don't! What a missed opportunity! Whether it's in a job interview, a pitch meeting, or a "negotiation" with your teenager about curfew, you should always expect a chance to ask a couple questions, so take the time to come up with some good ones. *Where did you see yourself in five years when you started with the company? What were some of the specific snags you hit as you tried to bring your product to market? What are you and your friends getting up to after 11 p.m.?* . . . Find a way to show that you've put some thought into the topic under discussion, in a way that puts it out there that you're thorough and forward-thinking. (Plus, it'd be helpful to know the answers to some of these questions, right?) We've all heard that old saying about how there's no such thing as a stupid question, but that's not really true. I've heard some pretty stupid questions, but the stupidest question in a negotiation is the one you never get around to asking. Sure, it might be that you don't ask a question because you're nervous or really unprepared, but I might also read a little more into it if I'm the one doing the interviewing. I might think you're not being totally honest with me if I give you an opportunity to dig a little deeper into what me or my company is about.

3. Come prepared with answers.

Same goes for the flip side to this question-and-answer business. You can probably anticipate four or five questions you're likely to get, so why not work on your answers ahead of your meet? *Why do you want this job? What can your product add to this market? Why can't I stay out an extra hour on the weekends?* Write those answers down, rehearse them into the ground, commit them to memory. If those questions don't come up, no biggie. But if they do, you'll be able to answer them intelligently, without hesitation.

4. Learn everything you can about the company you're pitching, the company you're hoping to work for, the product you're looking to sell.

Last thing you want in a negotiation is to come across

as out of your league. Next to last thing is to let the other person think you're not prepared, or you don't know what the hell you're talking about. So know what the hell you're talking about.

5. Consider your deal-breakers in advance.

We've all got our breaking points. Sometimes a deal isn't meant to happen. Maybe the terms just don't work for you, or you can't see a way to collaborate or give up control. You need to know these breaking points going in, because when your bottom line is firm you can stand on top of it.

6. Think in best-case scenarios.

What do you want out of this deal? What's the most you can ask for, the most you can hope for? Consider the ideal situation and see if there's a way to frame it so that it can also be seen as the ideal situation for the other person. If you're able to think this through beforehand and find a way for those ideal situations to match up, you'll be better positioned to make them so.

POWER FACT Know your stuff—up and down, and across the board. And know that if you invest your time in prep work before heading into a meeting or a pitch or a job interview, you won't be alone. A study reported by nego-tiations.com revealed that 40 percent of the time we spend in a negotiation is internal—meaning, where we dig deep and learn everything we can about the opposite party, so that when we do finally get to the table to make something happen, we're well and fully prepared.

Chapter 8

SET THE TONE

In any negotiation, your presentation is key. The way you dress, the way you accessorize, the way you speak . . . even the way you make eye contact or cross your legs or fold your arms can help you make or emphasize your point in a meaningful way.

And it's not just what you're putting out that can set the tone in a negotiation, it's what you're taking in . . . *everything* you're taking in. When I enter a room for an important meeting, all five senses are firing.

SIGHT: I take in the scene, and make a mental note of everything that might lend insight about the person or people I'm negotiating with. If I'm in someone else's office, that means checking out how it's decorated, noting what personal items or professional honors are on display, seeing if the room is neat and professional. If the person I'm meeting with is trying to make a statement with his or her surroundings, I want to make sure I "hear" it. If I'm the one hosting the meeting, I put myself in the other person's shoes and imagine them doing the same thing. I want to know what my digs say about me before I invite someone onto my turf.

SOUND: Noise level matters. Is there music playing in the background? Are we meeting in a crowded space where I'm going to need to raise my voice to be heard? What about if it's *too* quiet? Don't know about you, but I'm not a big fan of hearing myself think—though I do often wish I could hear what the other guy is thinking!

TOUCH: This won't apply in every situation, but it was all-important when most of my time was spent in and around fashion. I don't mean this in a creepy kind of way. What I mean is, fashion's a very tactile industry, it's often all about the feel of a fabric against your skin, which is why a lot of our meetings would start in a showroom where I'd spend some time touching the goods on display. The same goes in technology and certain types of product design; you want to be able to play with whatever item you're talking about—you know, take it out for a test run.

SMELL: I don't want to sound gross or juvenile, but sometimes I step into a room and there's a funky odor I just can't ignore. It gets in my nose and then it gets in my head and I start to think, How the hell can this person not notice this smell? Of course, on the opposite end are those times when you're struck by a soothing scent like lavender or citrus or eucalyptus or anything that's supposed to help you relax or create a certain mood. When I'm in someone else's office and I notice they've taken the time to create a special environment in this way, it signals to me that I'm dealing with someone thoughtful, who's set on being focused and present.

TASTE: This one comes into play when you're meeting over drinks, or a meal, and the other person is doing the ordering. Do they show consideration by asking about your dietary restrictions or preferences? Do they order the cheapest thing on the menu, or the most expensive? Or maybe you're meeting over a conference table and you're taking a bite of one of the pastries they've left out for you. Is that donut stale? Does the coffee taste like it was brewed last week? You can learn a lot about someone by the way they care for and feed their guests, so even if I'm not hungry I'll check out the spread.

A lot of times, we've got all this information coming at us, all at once, before we even shake hands with the other person. So there's a lot going on. When I was just starting out, I would take in all these sensations without even thinking about them, but **the *powershift* comes in knowing how what I'm seeing, hearing, touching, smelling, and tasting might come into play in the negotiation ahead.** Sometimes it does, sometimes it doesn't, but I want to be prepared.

SLOW YOUR ROLL

Okay, so let's say we've seen what there is to see, heard what there is to hear . . . the scene is set, and now it's time to get down to business. Here is where all the little signals and personality quirks we put out into the world can work for us or against us.

Take the time to pay close attention to the other party's behavior. For example, if they are speaking fast or at a high volume, that probably means they're overly enthusiastic, maybe a little too eager to do a deal.

On the flip side, when people are hesitant or uncertain, they will speak slowly, often at a low volume, and it could indicate that you're dealing with a reluctant customer— what the people on Capitol Hill these days might call a "hostile witness."

I try to be aware of these behaviors whenever I sit down with someone, because they can tell me a lot about the other person's enthusiasm or uncertainty, whatever the case may be. Research conducted by Albert Mehrabian shows that *only 7 percent* of what we communicate has to do with what we say. I'll tell you what makes up the other 93 per- cent later on, but for now I want you to start paying atten- tion to things like whether or not the other person's arms are crossed, which can be an indication that they're closed off to what I'm saying—or if they're leaning in as I speak, which can be an indication that they're especially inter- ested in what I'm saying. Don't just take my word for it, though. In a study conducted by Inc. of over two thousand negotiations, reporters found that no successful deal was made in any of the negotiations where one or both parties crossed their arms and legs.

As someone who's sat on the *Shark Tank* panel for the past eleven years, I've learned a little bit about how some of my fellow Sharks change their tone or their body language when they get excited about a deal—and about the ways some of our wannabe entrepreneurs signal their commitment or enthusiasm as well. Of course, the way things are set up on the show, it's not like this is a natural negotiating environment. There are dozens of people hanging around, more than a dozen cameras pointed at you, harsh studio lights meant to pick up every blemish or out-of-place hair. Plus, there's a script everyone's meant to follow as we get going. The deal is, the entrepreneurs are supposed to talk for the first two minutes. They've rehearsed that part of their pitch into the ground, even run it by the producers, but after that the gloves come off and we're back and forth and all over the place, depending on how the Sharks take the bait . . . or don't. Plus, almost every pitch begins the same way: The entrepreneur makes that long walk to the panel and greets the Sharks and starts to tell their story. What you see on the air is a heavily edited version of the pitch, so it might seem like we run through each one in ten or fifteen minutes, but in some cases the unedited pitch can run to an hour or two, or longer.

What's interesting here is that the crew is usually setting the shot for a couple minutes before the pitch actually begin —getting the lighting just right, or setting the stage. This can be an awkward few moments for the entrepreneurs, before they're technically "on" and the cameras are running, but I use that time to begin forming an opinion about each presenter. You have to realize, we're not supposed to speak to them, and they're not supposed to speak to us—but still, there are some interesting tells. If their hands are in their pockets, or they're shifting about nervously, I can see that they're uncomfortable, maybe underconfident. I *get* that— it's an intimidating room, an intimidating setup. And yet sometimes, entrepreneurs might be self-aware enough to know that all eyes are on them, so they'll look to smooth things over by turning to the panel and saying something like, "Whoa, so this is pretty awkward, huh?"

A line like that, a gesture like that, it always goes into the plus column for me, because I believe it shows a certain purity, a strength of character. It tells me that this person is genuine, someone I might want to do business with, and it's a big contrast with the people who come onto the show in what they think is a kind of power stance. They're all business, super-serious. Their hands will be by their sides, their feet will be open, and they'll just look straight at us Sharks while all this busy work production-type stuff is going on. Now, to give these people the benefit of the doubt, it's possible they're just nervous and this is how they handle their nerves, so I try not to hold it against them or let it shape my opinion before the pitch even begins—but at the same time, they don't earn any points with me the way they might if they tried to defuse the tension in the room by acknowledging it in a simple, human way.

One thing it helps to remember is that the people who

come on the show feel like they already know us—but for the Sharks on the panel, we don't know the first thing about the entrepreneurs about to pitch. We don't even get a fact sheet or backgrounder on them. What that means is that most of them have an idea in their heads of which Shark might offer the best fit, or who might be the most receptive to a deal. That's kind of what happened with Charlynda Scales, when she came on to pitch her special sauce thinking I'd respond on a personal level to her story and it worked out that I wasn't even scheduled to be on the panel that day. What you'll see a lot of the time is entrepreneurs subconsciously catering their pitch to a specific Shark. Maybe they'll be turned in such a way that they're mostly facing Robert at one end of the panel, or Mark at the other. Maybe they'll make eye contact with Lori, if they're talking about an innovative product they believe is in her wheelhouse. Maybe they'll lean in toward Barbara, if it's a play meant for her—and I suppose there are even some occasions when someone will target Kevin on a pitch, so they'll look directly at him.

Now, the way the show is set up, it's not just a Shark-versus-entrepreneur dynamic—there's also a Shark-versus-Shark dynamic that comes into play. I've learned over the years to study my fellow Sharks and get a good read on their level of interest before anyone makes an offer or bows out of a deal. With Robert, he'll tend to cross his legs in a way that leaves him open to the room when he's interested in a deal—and he'll cross them the other way if he's not. Also, he has this thing he does after he asks a question on a deal he's not keen on pursuing. He'll ask the question and then immediately close this portfolio notebook he always has with him on the set. Sometimes he'll even drop the book to his side as he asks the question—never a good sign for the entrepreneur, but sometimes a good sign for me if it's a deal I'm interested in and I'm worried about having to go up against Robert with my offer.

When Mark wants in on a deal, he's got this habit of leaning back in his chair, with his legs spread wide—like he's putting it out there that he's relaxed, and welcoming, and ready to take this on. When a pitch is not for him, you'll see him sit up a little straighter.

One of Lori's tells is she wraps her hair around her ears as she looks down to study her notes—almost like she's slipping into studious mode.

Kevin is hard to read. He likes and dislikes everyone equally. In all these years I haven't really been able to figure him out. A lot of times, it feels to me like he's making an offer just to take a stab at things. He's all about the money, and he always says as much, so I have never been able to catch him changing things up when the rest of us might be responding to a pitch in a personal way.

Barbara seems to tilt her head back a little bit when she's open to pursuing a deal—her own version of a welcoming pose.

I started paying attention to this stuff in Season Two, after Mark joined the show, and it felt to me like I had to up my game a little bit. Those first couple years, I went at deals one-on-one, not really thinking if there was another Shark chasing the same deal. But I started to realize that this type of approach put me at a disadvantage, because a lot of times I'd find myself in a bidding war that didn't really serve my interests.

ACCEPT THAT SIZE DOESN'T ALWAYS MATTER

Before I let my fellow Sharks off the hook, I want to spend some time sharing some of Mark Cuban's insights on negotiating, because I think they're relevant here. I've always thought that it had to be tough for a team owner to negotiate directly with a professional athlete. In the NFL or the NBA especially, you're dealing with these outsized physical specimens who can *really* fill a room, and it can be an intimidating thing to try to use your leverage with one of those guys staring you down.

Of course, this observation doesn't account for the fact that the athlete and the owner are almost never alone in a room banging out the terms of their next mega-deal—they've got their agents and general managers to deal with that. And it also ignores the fact that it could just as easily be the owner's outsized wallet that stands as the most intimidating variable in this scenario. **You never know what people are going to respond to, but it's interesting to think about the ways size or position might influence a deal.** That's why you used to get this old-school advice about trying to set up your meetings on your turf—in your office, maybe, or in a favorite restaurant—so you can get a kind of home-field advantage, and why some bosses used to furnish their office so that their desk chairs were higher than the visitor chairs. In that type of setup, it's all about the intimidation factor, but I never liked the idea of bullying someone into a deal. Manipulation isn't really my style: **I'd much rather bring someone around to my way of thinking on the strength of my ideas or the power of my personality.**

I had a chance to ask Mark about this when he agreed to sit down with me for this book. As most readers know, Mark isn't *just* one of the panelists on *Shark Tank*. He's also a wildly successful tech entrepreneur, and the billionaire owner of NBA basketball team the Dallas Mavericks. I run with a crowd that's big into basketball, which means I tag along to games from time to time, so when we started working together I was constantly pumping Mark with questions about the game and the unique place he seems to have made for himself within it. What a lot of people forget is that when Mark bought a majority stake in the Mavericks in January 2000 he was just forty-one years old—one of the youngest owners in the league. At first, he tells me, he was careful not to upset the culture or make any waves when he went to league meetings, but if you know Mark you'll know *that* didn't last very long.

"I stood out like a sore thumb," he tells me of those first meetings with his fellow owners. "Everyone wore suits. They were very straitlaced. When I got there, it was a rubber-stamp meeting. There was an agenda, everyone voted yes, and they ended quickly. I remember asking the commissioner, David Stern, if we were allowed to ask questions, and

I think he regrets to this day telling me that we could. From there, everything changed. What happens today is one hundred and eighty degrees from how it was when I got there."

To hear Mark tell it, the NBA is a players' league, meaning the power rests with the athletes on the court, not with the owners writing the checks. This is most apparent in negotiations with a franchise, name-above-the-title player. For most of Mark's time as owner of the Mavericks, the team's star was Dirk Nowitzki, the future Hall of Famer from Germany, who for the most part was able to dictate his terms whenever his contract came up. Part of the reason for this is the league's collective bargaining agreement, which offers "max" slots for veteran superstar players, so in a lot of ways an owner like Mark has his hands tied when a top player is facing free agency—meaning that if you don't pay a player the very top dollar amount allowed by the league, he can sign with another team for a slightly lesser amount that is also determined by the league. In other words, when sitting down to negotiate salaries, it's on the owner to shift the power over to their side of the table, and in Mark's case that means creating the kind of corporate culture that can serve as a magnet. He tells me that when he or his management team has been unable to set the right tone with employees it has come back to bite him, and when they get it right it has propelled them to the top of the industry.

MARK CUBAN, on finding a way to set the tone in a negotiation by creating a winning environment and a culture of inclusion: "The NBA is a star-driven league. That is why we are so popular globally, and why we are becoming more and more connected to pop culture and kids than any other pro sport. Fans know players from top to bottom of our rosters. So when a superstar like Dirk wants to negotiate, he truly has all the leverage. That said, it's my job as owner, whether it's Dirk or Luka Doncic or any other player, to make sure they want to stay part of the organization. The same applies to any of my companies. Turnover is always expensive. The happier our employees are, the less turnover there is and the better the results."

Mark's comments here remind me that setting a tone in a negotiation isn't just about learning to read people's body language and paying attention to the signals you're putting out. **It's about creating a culture and a welcoming environment that people want to be a part of.** That's why you see a lot of entrepreneurs on *Shark Tank* lose their *shit* when Mark lets it be known that he wants to be in business with them, because people get that he's a good and loyal and innovative partner. They gravitate toward him. It's like there's a force field surrounding him as he moves about the set, and people pick up on that because they know he's not out there trying to take advantage of anybody. He might not be the most physically imposing presence in a room, but sometimes your reputation—your character—is more important than whether or not your chair is raised, or you cross your arms a certain way, or you raise your voice when you don't get what you want.

That said, there are certain physical behaviors you'll want to pay attention to if you expect to be taken seriously in a negotiation.

I'll hit just a few of them here:

1. Look the other person in the eye.

Meaningful eye contact is important, but to my thinking it's not nearly as important as what it tells me when someone is constantly avoiding it. My mother always taught me to look the other person in the eye when I was speaking, but you'd be amazed at how many people can't follow this one basic rule. I know this is the kind of stuff that sometimes seems so obvious—but clearly it isn't obvious to the person who isn't doing it! There are some people who whether they realize this is what they're doing or not only make eye contact with the highest-status or most senior person in the room. This is a mistake. The eye contact rule applies to everyone from the CEO to his or her assistant (and trust me, that assistant has influence!). In a related point, let me also state the obvious: Don't be looking at your phone, or your watch, during an important meeting. Nothing says *disinterest* like people checking their devices like they've got someplace else they need to be or something else jockeying for their attention.

2. Perfect the "three bears" handshake—not too limp, not too hard, but just right.

Again, this might sound obvious, and you've definitely heard it before. But it's worth repeating—that wet-noodle handshake can kill a deal before it even has a chance to happen. When you shake someone's hand in greeting, there should be some muscle behind it . . . but don't overdo it. If you just kind of hang there and let the other person do the shaking, you'll come across as soft. But if you pump away like you're trying to draw water, you'll be seen as too aggressive. Try to land somewhere in the middle on this. And if you happen to be one of those people who suffer from sweaty palms, do yourself a favor and discreetly wipe your hand against your pant leg before shaking.

3. Speak in complete sentences.

No hemming and hawing, please. Give fully formed answers in response to all questions. Don't know about you, but it bugs me when someone can't quite seem to finish a thought. It tells me they can't find the words, or don't have the patience to try to make themselves understood. When I'm thinking about working with someone, I'm thinking about how they will represent me or my brand, and so of course I'm drawn to people who are thoughtful and articulate and able to communicate effectively. Of course, this matters less in the case of informal conversations, but in general, you want to show that you're in the habit of thinking before you speak.

4. Let the other person speak in complete sentences.
Always remember that the person across the table is trying to make their case as well, so don't interrupt. There should be a natural give-and-take to your negotiation, but that means *giving* the other person a chance to talk and *taking* the time to think things through before you open your mouth. As I mentioned earlier, there's valuable information encoded in whatever the other person has to say, so don't risk missing something important by insisting on being the one who dominates the conversation. Of course, the other reason you don't want to cut someone off is because most of the important information you're likely to hear will come at the end of someone's pitch. People tend to build up to making their main point, so if you jump in too soon you might never hear it.

5. Be aware of your facial expressions.
I'm told I have a lousy poker face. Chances are you do, too. As a species we're wired to wear our emotions on our faces, even though we're rarely aware of it. So spend some time in front of a the mirror and see how your expressions signal your emotions. Even better, try this quick exercise: Set up your phone to record a brief video as you read aloud from the Twitter feed of

someone who irritates the hell out of you. Then do the same thing as you read from the feed of someone you admire. Take a look at some of the subtle and not-so-subtle differences in your expression and see if you can do a better job of hiding your true feelings on a second pass.

POWER FACT Just how important is body language? Well, if you study the work of Dr. Albert Mehrabian of UCLA, one of the leading psychologists in the field of nonverbal communication, it's damn near everything. According to Dr. Mehrabian's research, our words represent only 7 percent of what we communicate to another person. The tone of our voice accounts for 38 percent of what we put across . . . and the rest (55 percent!) comes through in how we carry ourselves, in how we present ourselves, and in our facial expressions.

Chapter 9

MAKE THE FIRST MOVE

One of the oldest rules of thumb in negotiating is that you're supposed to let the other person fire the first shot. The idea is to let them throw out a number and establish a kind of floor, so you don't make the mistake of maybe starting off a negotiation with a set of terms that might be *way* lower than what you could have gotten if you'd just shut up and waited for an opening offer.

Clearly, you never want to be negotiating against yourself, but I've never bought in to this line of thinking. Here's why: **When you set your terms at the outset, you're able to anchor the conversation in a way that serves you and your interests.** As we covered earlier, if you've done your homework you'll know how an acceptable deal might look. You'll have a general framework in your head, so as long as you start somewhere between what you'd settle for and what you'd hope for, you're doing okay.

On *Shark Tank,* the way it's set up, the people who come in to do the pitch are always the ones to set the terms. That's the format of the show, to have people come in with their ask on the table, so using old-school logic the Sharks are always at an advantage, but I don't see it that way. Instead, when I hear a pitch from entrepreneurs who have taken a balanced view of their business and come up with a fair evaluation and a forecast of expectations that seems in line with recent sales, I'm impressed. It leaves me inclined to think that these people know their stuff and are looking for a genuine collaboration. If it's a business or partnership I'm interested in pursuing and believe I can add value to, I'll be more inclined to make an offer in this scenario because I'll get the message straightaway that the people I'm dealing with are diligent and reasonable and professional. They're not looking to play games. It's when those valuations have no basis in reality that I begin to have some trouble, but if you start from a place of reason you can almost always keep the conversation going.

That's what a negotiation is all about, really— keeping the conversation going. If you start off with a number that makes no sense, or projections that are based on a fantasy, there's no reason to keep talking. The same goes if I'm the one making the pitch and I decide to wait for a suitor to make me an offer, the way conventional wisdom has always suggested. But I don't always have the time to wait around to see if somebody's going to make me an offer, so I like to be the one to get things cooking. The sooner I get to determine if somebody's trying to lowball me, or to disregard the hard work I've put into something, the sooner I can set my sights on the next deal.

Another thing I like about setting the terms in a deal is that it puts it out there that you know your value, and that you're not interested in hearing from someone else what *they* think you're worth. After all, that's what we ask our entrepreneurs to do on *Shark Tank,* so I figure I should play by the same rules—as long as I do it from a place of integrity.

This integrity piece is key, because there has got to be a reasonable expectation that an established set of terms is rooted in . . . well, in *reason.* This applies every time you're looking to bring two sides together on a deal. Here's an example: Think back to the last time you shopped for a car. The dealer sets the price and establishes the tone for the conversation that may or may not follow, and you can bet that number will be consistent with the pricing at other dealerships in the area. If the number is unreasonably high compared with what's on the market, the customer will walk. Game over.

Making the first move in a negotiation also allows you to control the narrative. Good negotiating is all about good storytelling, and if you let somebody else try to tell your story you'll never get the message out in just the right way. Or maybe you will, but you'll get there by accident instead of by design, so why hang back and let someone else tell you how things are going to go when they're much more likely to go your way if you're the one setting the terms? Even more, when you hang back in this way, you'll be better able to pick your spots and offer up a reasonable counterproposal—because, let's face it, people want to feel like you're meeting them halfway.

SHORT STEPS, LONG VISION

My friend Pitbull, the Miami-based rapper, has done a great job controlling the narrative over the years—but there was a time in there when it wasn't clear he'd even get a chance to tell his own story.

If you know Pit's music, you might know a little bit of his background. He grew up on the streets of Miami with a fighter's mentality. His parents were from Cuba, and out of that he had this mindset that nothing would be handed to him. Nothing was easy. He had to hustle for every edge. Matter of fact, he took the stage name Pitbull because when a pit bull bites down it bites down hard. It doesn't back down, doesn't let go. It's constantly on the attack—that's the way Pit learned to approach life.

Here, let him tell it: "I was literally like a pit bull in a cage, ready to get out and do what I know how to do, which is hustle."

The Miami that Pitbull grew up in back in the '80s and '90s was the cocaine capital of the world. Those streets were hard, man. Everyone he knew had a brother or a father or an uncle in prison, or maybe they'd been killed, or maybe they'd been forced to snitch so now they were facing a whole other hassle while their families were made to live under that dark cloud. And then, at the living-large end of things, you even had people who somehow climbed to the top of the drug trade and turned it into an empire, so they were out there moving about the city like nothing could touch them or push them from their place on the throne.

Pit, whose real name is Armando Christian Pérez, grew up around all of that, and he took it all in. First time we met, we connected because we were a lot alike. We'd both been determined to sidestep the fate of so many of our friends in our neighborhoods. We'd each tried to fly under the radar, stay out of trouble, keep our focus on making money with our side hustles, instead of slinging dope or jacking cars. In Pit's case, he was mowing lawns, working construction, even running his own dry-cleaning business for a stretch. And then, when he got into the rap game, he took all kinds of heat for it—just like I caught flak for making clothes. People wrote us off for being *soft,* or fancy, or whatever—but whatever we were, whatever we weren't, we weren't soft. No way. We were just hard in different ways.

We knew our own minds.

The key thing we had in common was that neither one of us was willing to wait for something to happen *to* us . . . or *for* us. We were each out to make something happen, and the way we did that was to make the first move. Always.

We saw what we wanted and we rose to grab at it—hey, what other choice did we have?

When Pit was trying to make some noise with his music, he'd show up wherever his boys were at and hand out his mix tapes. Back then, this was what you had to do to make it in the music business. You had to be *heard*. He tells me now he used to think of it like his own version of the dope game. He was just peddling a different product, that's all, trying to turn people on to his rap.

Sometimes it's tough to be heard, and this is especially true in certain communities, for certain groups of disenfranchised kids. Like I said, we were a lot alike, me and Pit. We both struggled in school—me because of my dyslexia, and Pit because he just didn't see the point. He couldn't even be bothered to go, unless it was basketball season. He had to keep his grades up to play ball, so the motivation was built in, but once the clock ran out on the season he barely went to class.

Lucky for Pit he had a teacher who believed in him—or at least wasn't so quick to write him off. Her name was Hope Martinez, and she really made the difference. She caught him skipping a couple times and instead of reporting him, she tried to reason with him, talking about the importance of sticking in school and all that. She saw something in him—maybe because once they got to talking she could see how he was wired, how he was determined to make something of himself, in his own way.

When he told me this story, I kind of loved that this teacher's name was Hope—a lot of times that's what it comes down to when you've got a kid who could easily make a turn onto a wrong road. **When you hope for the best for someone, you make it possible for them to tap the best in themselves**—and here it worked out that this one teacher was able to give this one student who wanted to be a rapper a reason to think his dream was within reach.

Take the one time, after Pit and the teacher had gotten to know each other a little bit, and trust each other a little bit, she stepped out into the schoolyard to break up what looked to be a fight. All these kids were circled 'round, and as she worked her way through the crowd she saw Pit in the middle of the circle, locked in an epic freestyle battle. Yeah, something was going down, but it wasn't exactly what this teacher originally thought. She stood for a while and listened. Then she stepped back and checked out the crowd of kids—laughing, cheering, totally into it.

"After, she come up to me and said, 'You know what? You got talent,'" Pit says. "And I was like, 'Aw, come on, Miss Martinez.' But she was like, 'Nah, nah, you got talent. For real.'"

Because this one teacher believed in him, Pit started to believe in himself, and somewhere along the way he managed to build up a pile of positive reinforcement that told him he was onto something.

Only, it wasn't any one thing, it was everything.

What I admire about Pit and the way he came to his music and found his moment was that he didn't ask for permission to do his thing. He didn't check out the scene and do what was acceptable, what was expected. He listened to his own inner voice and then he put that voice out into the world in a way that moved him, in a way that served him. In other words, he made the first move—even when that move had him breaking the rules.

"We have a saying in Spanish," he tells me. " 'Pasos cortos, vista larga,' which means 'Short steps, long vision.' And when you're living in a world where it's instant gratification, because you're making easy money, quick money, you've got to always watch out for that, which is why I always say, 'Dope money comes quick, leaves quicker.' For me, it's slow but fo' sho', you know. It's a marathon, not a sprint, always."

With Pitbull, like it is with a lot of dynamic personalities I've been blessed to know, his success came from placing himself on a purposeful path. He saw a way up and out of his circumstances and he rose to meet it, even knowing he'd have to play the long game to do so. In his case, the lift came from music. In mine, it came from fashion. In yours—who knows? Maybe your thing is real estate, or app design, or podcasting. Maybe you're good with numbers, or you have a great eye behind a camera, or a way with words. Point is, **when you're out in front—as an artist, an innovator, a change agent, or whatever—you sometimes need to make that first move.**

But what you should also be learning is *when and how* to make the first move—because **if you wait for that move to find you . . . well, you might be kept waiting forever.** Or somebody else's idea of what's good for you will be allowed to take hold, and you'll be operating off *that* instead of what you originally had in mind.

So go with what you know, trust your instincts, take your best shot . . . and whatever you do, don't be caught waiting for somebody else to give you permission to do your thing.

PITBULL, on reading the situation: "You deal with a lot of these guys in these major corporations, they don't have that street intuition. You have to live it. You grow up like I did, you learn to read plays. I can look at someone's eyes and tell you if I'm going to do business with this person or not. A handshake tells me a lot about a person. And it's not just these guys at the top who give themselves away. It's the kids coming up. Everybody's so programmed now. It's like, there's no way a twenty-two-year-old kid, who's on his phone all the time, who's always communicating, can have this kind of knowledge, this kind of wisdom, this kind of maturity. He's so connected, he's disconnected. He can't read plays. His eyes, his face, they're buried in his phone, so he's not even aware of his surroundings. He's nowhere."

I want to circle back here to the story I started telling earlier about the *powershift* that took me from FUBU to *Shark Tank*. When Mark Burnett came calling to pitch me on the idea of signing on to this little show he was developing, I wasn't entirely sold on the concept. Yeah, the show was a hit in these other markets all over the world, but I wasn't feeling it here at home, didn't think American audiences would respond to it in the same way, so it wasn't even clear to me that this would be anything more than a one-shot deal. Plus, what the producers were offering didn't sound all that appealing. The money wasn't great, on either a per-episode or a season-long basis, but the more troubling piece of the deal was that they expected me to invest in these start-ups with my own money.

I shot back with something stupid like "Wait, if I'm going Hollywood, *I'm* supposed to get paid, not the other way around."

Then, when they started listing some of the other Sharks they were lining up to be on the show, I thought they were selling me on a lineup they didn't really have. When I heard Mark Cuban's name, for example, I couldn't believe a guy like that would carve out the time from his busy schedule to take a flier on a show like this, especially if it meant he'd have to use his own money to make something happen on a deal. The guy was a billionaire, and he was already getting a bunch of television time as the owner of the Dallas Mavericks, throwing chairs onto the court when he didn't like a call against his team.

But I don't want to get too far away from my decision to sign on. I was curious, thought a regular role on a show like *Shark Tank* might serve me in pursuit of my television goals. No, it wasn't any kind of lucrative network gig, but in success I saw that it could offer me a platform to pivot into something new, to vault me to a place where I could start telling a different story. Trouble was, success in this arena wasn't guaranteed—and from where I sat, it didn't even seem all that likely.

Ultimately, I decided to do the pilot, because I never really thought the show would get picked up, and because I figured if I went out to LA to do the taping I could at least sit down with Mark Burnett and pitch him these three smoking-hot ideas I had for shows of my own. **That's how it goes sometimes: You take one deal because you think it might lead you into the next one.** You walk through one open door because you think there's some other door waiting for you inside that next room, a door you might not even know about just yet. There's even a term for this in the retail trade—we call it a *loss leader.* It's the little thing that takes you to the next big thing, and we should be taking the same approach in our own lives and careers. No, I'm not suggesting we should sell ourselves short, but **every once in a while there's a move or an opportunity that doesn't feel exactly right on its face but holds out the promise of something completely new and exciting on the back of it.**

Sometimes getting out in front of an opportunity means anticipating a change in the marketplace before anyone else. That's kind of how things went down with Pit, when he pivoted into a whole new musical style. The way that happened was he was in the Dominican Republic and at a club heard a song called "World, Hold On," by the French deejay Bob Sinclar. He saw all these Dominican women dancing, grooving, having a big old time, even though they didn't speak a word of English, and he got it in his head to make music in a global way. This was back before all these world deejays like DJ Snake and Afrojack, and Steve Aoki and David Guetta, got on the same kick and you started seeing all these huge festivals. Pit found tremendous power in learning to think of music as a universal language. And because he was first to act on this, because he didn't sit back and wait for someone else to change things up *for* him, he was able to set the terms and lead the way—a *powershift* you could dance to! So read the play . . . create the framework . . . establish your terms . . . and set the story in motion in a way that serves you and your interests.

KEEP PERSPECTIVE

One of the hardest things to do in a negotiation is take the other person's view. But if you can find a way to imagine how the deal might look from the other side of the table, you'll be in a better position to get what you want—and if it works out that the other person gets what they want as well . . . well, that's the best of all possible outcomes.

After all, in a negotiation, it's all about making sure both sides are rewarded for their efforts. Think about what's in this deal . . . for you. Think about what's in this deal . . . for the other person. Think about the outcome you'd probably be seeking if your ego wasn't involved. And finally, think about what may or may not be going on with the person on the other side of the table. Make some room in your thinking for the possibility that they are having a bad day, or that there might be some stresses at home, or maybe even a looming health crisis that's got them thinking a certain way.

One way to look at it: **Negotiating is a lot like selling, except what you're peddling is yourself.** What I mean by that is, if you come at it from a place of trying to meet someone else's needs, a winning negotiation can help to fill the gap between what you're asking for and what you're prepared to give. This was another one of those insights I was able to figure out for myself. But now that I know what I know, looking back on it I can see that the way I look to meet the other person's needs is tied in to how I've always tried to meet my customer's needs, going back to when I first started selling products. Thing is, when you're out there grinding at an early age, when your street smarts are more useful to you than your book smarts, you learn to look to fill a need, whatever it is. And if you can't identify a *need* straightaway, then you've got to identify a *want* instead.

In a lot of ways, this mindset reminds me of the long run-up we had at *Shark Tank*. I've talked about this with Clay Newbill, the executive producer who was brought on to help develop the show for American audiences, after the format had been so successful in other countries. In the beginning, Clay's job was to watch every episode he could find of the UK and Canada versions because he believed audiences there most closely resembled American audiences. So he sat down and tried to figure out what it was that US viewers would want to see in a show like this—and, just as important, what entrepreneurs could expect to get out of the transaction. Without their enthusiastic participation, we would be nowhere, so we had to cater to them as well as to our viewers.

Clay studied the pacing of these other versions, the way they treated the entrepreneurs who came on to pitch their businesses or products, how those businesses performed after appearing on the show. In other words, he was doing his homework, setting the tone, preparing to make the first move. The idea, he says, was to play with the formula a little bit to make sure it would appeal to viewers, while at the same time positioning the show in such a way that small business owners and innovators would consider an appearance on *Shark Tank* a unique opportunity. Basically, he had to take in all these different perspectives: the network, the viewers, the entrepreneurs, the potential Sharks they were still in the process of auditioning. **There had to be something in it for everybody, or the show wouldn't work.**

The way it played out those first couple seasons, the quality of the pitches wasn't that great. Clay and the other producers will tell you it took a while to be able to identify businesses with interesting stories behind them, and to recruit colorful, engaging entrepreneurs willing to drop what they were doing to fly out to Los Angeles to be on our show, with no guarantees that they'd get a deal or even that they'd get on the air. It was a tough sell—and frankly, there were some kinks that still had to be worked out.

One of those kinks was the look and feel of the show. You'd be amazed how much thought went into this one element alone. For the pilot episode, just to give you an idea, they had the Sharks sitting at a huge desk on a platform about a foot higher than where the entrepreneurs were standing. It was sleek, professional, even kind of cool . . . but in the end, the look and feel of the set wasn't really working.

> CLAY NEWBILL, on getting the *Shark Tank* set just right: "In the pilot, there was more distance between the Sharks and the entrepreneurs. The color scheme was blue and white, with dramatic lighting. Everyone thought it looked great. But after taping completed, we started editing the material. We spent weeks looking at the set in the edit bays as we built the pilot episode, and during that time we realized that it felt off. The set lacked warmth. It felt like Superman's Arctic lair. Plus, the Sharks seated high up behind the desk made them feel inaccessible. The distance between them and the entrepreneurs was too great. We wanted the exchanges to be more intimate. After all, the entrepreneurs' stories and the heart they showed in pursuing their dreams should be shared in a more intimate setting."

As regular viewers of the show will know, we changed the look of the set completely after shooting the pilot—all because the producers were able to see the value in each point of view. It ended up that the producers changed the color scheme to make the set seem warmer, more inviting.

They brought the Sharks and the entrepreneurs at eye level, so everyone would feel more comfortable, like they were in this thing together.

End of the day, they stepped back from what they had built and tried to see if there was a better way to serve the many different perspectives that needed to be considered if the show was going to be successful.

CUT YOUR OWN TRAIL

Whenever I'm on the road, I try to carve out some time for myself away from the noise and hustle of my days. If I'm out in California, I'll go for a walk on the beach. If I'm in the heartland, I'll set off on a trek through town. And if I'm in the mountains I might park near a trailhead and start climbing.

This is where things get interesting. Most people, when they go for a hike, they follow a well-worn trail. They only discover the path everyone else has already walked. That's the safe way to play it. That's just like what happens when you let someone else set the terms in a negotiation. The safe way isn't always the best way, and it's almost never the most fun or exciting or surprising. But if you're out in front, you get to call the shots. I can't tell you how many times I've set off on an unmarked trail and come upon an out-of-the-way fishing spot that seems to be mine and mine alone. No one's around for miles. And I know I never would have found that spot if I'd followed someone else's trail—meaning, if I'd let them lead me to where *they* wanted me to go. That's just an example of the great riches that are out there waiting for you when you refuse to fall in behind someone else.

So go ahead and lead the way, and if you don't quite know where to start here are a few things to keep in mind:

1. Remember that this is your story to tell.

When you let others frame the terms of a deal, you allow them to frame the terms of your story. Start in with integrity, from a place of purpose, and you'll be in a better position to tell it like it is.

2. Create a clear time line in your mind on how the deal will progress going forward.

When your ask is accompanied by a clear set of goals laid out on a clear timetable, you let the other person know that you've spent some time thinking things through. They might spark to the idea of a certain level of growth being achieved by a target date, a target you won't be able to meet unless you're able to move forward on your terms.

3. Know the outcome that makes sense for you.

Anything less and it's not worth your time; anything more and it'll feel like you're getting away with something. It's never fun to build a partnership on a one-sided deal, even if the deal is weighted in your favor. Be on the side of right instead.

4. Acknowledge the history.

It might be that you've been down this road before. It might be that the people on the other side of the table have been down this road before. Don't ignore the elephant in the room. If you've worked together before and things didn't go well, be the first to bring it up, and be honest in your assessment about what went wrong and what you expect to be able to change this time around. Here again, it's the party that waits for the other to start a difficult conversation that will be on its heels.

5. Be prepared to walk away.

This applies to every deal, of course. But it is especially important when you're the one out in front, opening the conversation. We all have our breaking points. Know yours before starting in.

POWER FACT I'm not the only one who thinks making the first move in a negotiation is your strongest play. According to the Harvard Law School Daily Blog, researchers at Duke, the University of Michigan, and the University of Houston determined that negotiators who made the first move did better in purely economic terms than those who did not. The flip side to this was that they also reported feeling more anxiety than their counterparts. But I'm thinking that's probably because they'd been conditioned to think they were making some kind of fool move by firing the opening shot. Trust the numbers on this one.

Chapter 10

PLAY TO WIN–WIN

O kay, so now that we've got the perspective thing down, let's take a look at what we should do with it. I mean, it's one thing to just consider where the other person is coming from; it takes a certain mindset to put it into play.

Without this mindset, we'd never get to some of the stories *Shark Tank* viewers still talk about—like one of the most moving and memorable pitches in the show's history, which is worth revisiting here for the way it shows what can happen when everyone's interests are served in a deal. It was a pitch made by the three children of a New York City firefighter who had recently passed away from a cancer he developed from being a first responder at Ground Zero following the attacks on September 11, 2001. The firefighter's name was Keith Young, and his dream was to come on our show to pitch a product he'd developed called the Cup Board Pro, a kitchen cutting board that had a built-in detachable cup to make it easy to clean up after chopping fruits and veggies. It was one of those clever products designed to meet a household need we didn't even realize we had—and so in this one way, at least, it was a lot like your everyday *Shark Tank* pitch. But in another way, it stands as a powerful illustration of what can happen when *all* sides in a negotiation come out ahead.

There were five of us Sharks on the set that day—me, Mark Cuban, Lori Greiner, Kevin O'Leary, and guest Shark Matt Higgins—and I think every one of us was in tears when this firefighter's kids started telling us their story. Their names were Kaley, Christian, and Keira, and they hadn't lost *just* their father—their mother, Beth, had passed away, too, after being diagnosed with stage IV breast cancer. This poor family had been through hell, but these kids were determined and resilient. They were able to stand in front of us with smiles and tons of energy. And best of all, in purely deal terms, they seemed to know their stuff, which was important because they were running the company. They lit up when they shared their father's story. After his wife's death, Keith Young was left to take care of their three young kids, and he developed a love for cooking. He'd already pulled his share of kitchen duty at the firehouse, and it turned out the guy could cook! He'd been a two-time winner on the cooking competition show *Chopped,* and he'd written a cookbook called *Cooking with the Firehouse Chef,* but once he came up with the idea for this cutting board he kept talking about coming on the show and trying to turn it into a business.

Turned out he pushed that dream all the way to an audition tape he'd prepared for our show's producers a couple months before he died, and Clay Newbill set it up so they showed a clip from that tape during the kids' pitch.

On its merits alone, the Young kids would have walked away with a deal for the Cup Board Pro. They'd come on the show seeking one hundred thousand dollars for a 10 percent stake in the business, and even without the heartstrings I have to think Lori would have jumped on this one because she does such a great job with these household-type products. But this pitch was as much about emotions as business, so all five of us on the panel decided to go in on the deal and at the same time we pledged to give back any profits to a charity helping firefighters suffering from 9/11-related illnesses.

Now, a story like this, we couldn't exactly treat it like any other deal on the show. This was one of those feel-good stories that tugged at your heartstrings and you couldn't help but be rooting for these kids to do well. Happily, they did. The inventor's kids got the deal they were looking for while raising awareness for the risks that heroes like their dad make every day. And, the people at home went crazy for the product, even as their hearts were broken by what these kids had gone through. By the next afternoon, we had back orders totaling more than a million dollars of sales—so clearly, the Young family touched something in our viewers, and it all flowed in some way from the many different interests we had to serve.

This pitch was a bit of an outlier for us at *Shark Tank*, but at the same time it stands as a compelling example of the power to be found in a transaction that serves multiple interests. **I'm a big fan of doing deals that make sense for both sides—let's call it a two-way** *powershift.*

On *Shark Tank* especially, I never want to be the guy who has his hands in the pockets of any of the entrepreneurs who come onto our set. There are obvious, strategic reasons for this that go beyond good karma and doing the right thing, although I'm also a big fan of good karma and doing the right thing. Clearly, if you get the better of someone on a deal, that person is not going to be someone you can call on in the future—plus, if the deal calls for that person to continue working with you in some way, they will be unlikely to invest themselves fully in a project or collaboration that doesn't reward them fairly. As far as I'm concerned, **it always pays to feed the machine that feeds you**—meaning, when you put good things into a deal on both sides, you'll get good things back in return.

One of the things I always try to do is to make it so I can call on the other person in a deal at a later date. If we're meant to continue working together, I need to be able to look them in the eye, share a meal with them, sing karaoke with them, work with them to push our project in a direction that serves us both—and hopefully, work with them in the future on a project neither one of us has even thought about just yet. As you read along, you'll see that this idea will follow us into Part III of the book, which is all about building relationships and making connections that last. For now, though, here's something to keep in mind: **On most deals, you should be looking to make a partner, not an adversary.** Some of my colleagues in the Tank don't always take the same view. I don't want to call them out in these pages, so I won't mention them by name here: You're welcome, Mr. Wonderful. (Hey, I never said anything about *nicknames*! Just joking, Kevin's a great guy, but sometimes he makes it too easy.)

That said, I don't mind trying to beat my fellow Sharks in a deal, because a lot of times we're in adversarial positions, chasing the same prize. We're operating on the same level playing field, with a lot of the same advantages, so I believe it's fair game for us to go at one another every once in a while. Frankly, that's one of the reasons people tune in, to see the in-fighting and jockeying for position that sometimes happens when we want in on the same deal. But **when I'm looking to invest in someone who's invested everything they have in a business or product, the last thing I want to do is come out ahead at someone else's expense.** That's no way to start a working partnership, right?

Truth is, a *Shark Tank* negotiation is just like any other negotiation—only it happens in front of a bunch of cameras, and at an accelerated pace. In real life, these kinds of conversations would happen over a week; on the show (to the viewers), they happen in minutes. It's basically a condensed, jam-packed version of what it's like to negotiate in the real world—also like the speed-dating version of negotiation. But even so, the general deal-making framework is the same. In most situations where a business is seeking capital, there's gonna be imbalance between what the entrepreneurs are bringing to the table and the resources investors have to offer. That imbalance is at the heart of the show. Typically, these entrepreneurs have their hands out. They're looking for some kind of edge, some much-needed capital, whatever the case may be. A lot of times they *need* to make a deal to keep their businesses going. Us Sharks aren't up against it in quite the same way. Yeah, we're out to make deals, and to keep the show interesting, and we're always looking at diversifying and finding creative ways to make a return on our investments, but the health of our portfolios or the strength of our deal flow doesn't depend on any one transaction. And so if we were to come out and bigfoot our way into a one-sided deal with an entrepreneur, it would in some ways negate the hard work that entrepreneur had put into their business, which had earned them a spot on the show in the first place.

Another thing: One-sided deals tend not to serve you in the long run. This isn't about being altruistic or celebrating the good karma that finds you in a win–win deal. At the end of the day, we're interested in making money and building a successful enterprise, so in purely business terms it makes sense to do deals that last.

The way I see it, my role on the show is not to deal from

strength. No, I believe it's my obligation on the show to deal from a place of integrity, from a place of collaboration, from a place of shared hopes and dreams, because once we shake hands on a deal with one of our entrepreneurs we're going to have to work together to make sure our partnership pays off. This applies to the deals I make in the Tank, as well as to the deals I make away from the show.

And so—for me, at least—the deal doesn't work unless it works both ways, and in order for *that* to happen you have to frame it in win–win terms from the very beginning, so that's where I'm coming from when I hear a pitch from one of our entrepreneurs on the show. And yet while we always make our best effort to close the deal that we made in the Tank, many times certain deal points are renegotiated once we're done taping. There are a bunch of reasons for this. First and foremost, the due diligence we complete after each segment is taped often turns up sales figures that don't really match the numbers we've heard during the pitch. Sometimes we discover something shady in the background of one of the entrepreneurs, or a side business we didn't know about that might leave us wondering if the principal will be able to devote their full attention to whatever it was that was pitched on the show. And sometimes there are competing market forces the entrepreneur wasn't able to see without bringing in an objective outsider's perspective.

A number of factors that go into these deals are unique to the *Shark Tank* experience, so as an investor I have some concerns I wouldn't necessarily have in a more typical pitch scenario. For one thing, we tape these shows in bunches. Typically, we tape for two weeks in June, and another two weeks in September, and there's about a three-month lag from the time our first segments are taped to when our first shows of the fall season make it onto the airwaves.

A lot can happen during those three months. A business can go bust . . . a competitor can beat a product to market . . . a much-needed patent application can be denied . . . an expected round of financing or a promised order from a major retailer can fall through.

One thing I want to point out here is that during the first few seasons, I didn't pay too much attention to what my partners were planning to do with my investment. They might have come on the set and said they needed an infusion of funds to meet the demands of production, or that they wanted to step up their marketing efforts, but in the end it worked out that the money was used to cover general operating expenses and perhaps even go toward an entrepreneur's salary or paying down debt. Or maybe it worked out that the idea was to use the money over time—on a certain schedule, once the business began to hit certain goals—but it somehow got tossed into a pool of funds that made it difficult for me to track exactly how it was being used.

I got better at this, a couple years in—and as I did I believe I became a better partner in these deals. Basically, I put a whole team in place to help me with the surge of *Shark Tank* deals that started flowing my way, and with it came a system designed to make sure everyone's interests were addressed before we ultimately threw in together. At each step along the way, I try to set things up so that it's easy to make the adjustments we need to honor the spirit of the deal we reached on the set.

GETTING READY FOR PRIME TIME

It's impossible for me to look at the win–win aspects of a deal I might make on the show without also considering some of the other factors at play in a *Shark Tank* pitch. A television studio, with the prospect of millions of people watching, is an unusual setting for a negotiation, and I hear from viewers and readers all the time who want to know what makes not only a good deal but also a good *Shark Tank* segment. I always tell them it depends . . .

- Sometimes, there's something unique about the business or product that is worth highlighting.

- Sometimes, there's a dramatic or empowering story behind the entrepreneur or innovator making the pitch.

- Sometimes, a pitch is so strong it sets off one of those feeding frenzies I just mentioned, where a bunch of Sharks want in on the deal.

- Sometimes, a pitch is so weak that viewers will tune in to watch a "spectacular fail," the same way rubber-neckers will slow down on the highway to look at a car crash.

We've been at this for over ten years, and I still have a tough time predicting which segments will make it onto the show. If I do a couple dozen deals over the course of a season, it's possible that only half of them will be featured. Sometimes a pitch doesn't make it because it's boring. Maybe it's too contentious—or not contentious enough. Maybe we're doing a Christmas episode, or a veterans-only episode, or a kids episode, and there are just too many segments featuring the same types of entrepreneurs.

What I try to do in the period of time between taping and when the lineup is announced is get through this due diligence phase with my partners, make sure we're in agreement on terms, and be honest with everybody about their chances of getting on the air. Typically, we won't know until three or four weeks ahead of time if one of our deals has made the cut, and when we get the good word we try to speed up the closing process to make sure all of our paperwork is in order. Depending on the business, we've got to make sure everything is in order on the production side as well, because as soon as that episode airs there's probably going to be a wave of orders coming in, and all kinds of promotional buzz.

The idea is to be good and ready for the *real* prime time.

PUT THOSE WIN–WINS IN THE WIN COLUMN

Now, one thing I hope I've made clear: I'm in these deals because I believe in the business, the product, the hole in the marketplace that needs filling. Sometimes I'm in a deal because I like what the entrepreneur is putting out there— I'm investing in them as much as I'm investing in their business. But once I decide to make an investment, I try to make a deal that makes sense for both parties.

So what does a win–win look like? Take the deal my friend and occasional *Shark Tank* colleague Bethenny Frankel negotiated for herself with her Skinnygirl cocktail lines. The transaction came on the back of a throwaway term Bethenny and her publisher used in the subtitle to her first book, *Naturally Thin: Unleash Your Skinnygirl and Free Yourself from a Lifetime of Dieting*—though of course she had no idea of the branding opportunity buried in that subtitle.

Just as an aside, I know how tough it is when you write a book to come up with the right subtitle. I've kicked around a bunch of them over the years, and a lot of times you're taking suggestions from the so-called experts in marketing, publicity, and editorial, as well as the people on your own team, but you never know when a word or phrase or idea might click. That's kind of what happened here.

At the time, coming off her first couple seasons on *The Real Housewives of New York,* Bethenny was probably best known as a natural food chef, and the book's title was meant to reinforce an emerging "Naturally Thin" brand. Now, just to be clear, the book was a big success in its own right. It was a *New York Times* bestseller, and it helped to establish Bethenny as a true media personality, but what's interesting to me in purely *powershift* terms was the way this Skinnygirl term took off. It was like that horse in the back of the pack that pulls ahead of the field on the homestretch. Nobody sees that horse coming, the smart money is elsewhere, but there it is overtaking the field.

Clearly, if Bethenny herself had believed this one word would be a game-changer for her, she would have used it somewhere in the title, but sometimes it works out that the true power in an enterprise is hidden at the outset.

Sometimes the market points out an area of strength you haven't even considered.

Bethenny followed that first book with a second—*The Skinnygirl Dish: Easy Recipes for Your Naturally Thin Life*—and you could see right there on the cover that the emphasis had flipped.

You know how radio stations used to run those "phrase that pays" promotions, dangling cash prizes to listeners who can identify a special word or phrase of the day when they get a call from the deejay? Well, Skinnygirl was the phrase that paid for Bethenny, and like any good businessperson she ran with it, hard. Within a couple years, she was out with a line of low-calorie Skinnygirl cocktails, and in the process she shook up the spirits industry. Nobody had really thought to make and market low-calorie mixers to women, and out of that it was only a matter of time before there were wines, flavored vodkas, and ready-to-drink cocktails.

When executives from Beam Global (the international spirits giant that's since become part of the Suntory conglomerate) started inquiring about the company, Bethenny negotiated a sweet little carve-out for herself that was pretty much unprecedented in a deal of this size—an epic *powershift,* when you break it down. What was so notable about that carve-out was not only that it was a huge benefit to Bethenny's bottom line *and* to her personal brand, going forward, but that it didn't really come at Beam's expense. The Skinnygirl name had no real value to them beyond the spirits category, so they were willing to let her keep it in order to get the deal they wanted. Without really realizing it, Bethenny stumbled on a classic win–win for herself and her new partners.

"I didn't know what I didn't know," she tells me now when I ask her how she managed to hold on to the Skinnygirl name for products beyond alcohol. Once there was all this buzz attached to the Skinnygirl name, her thinking was that she would continue to use it to develop a range of health, nutrition, fashion, and lifestyle items, and she didn't want to give all that up just because a single product category was now in play.

BETHENNY FRANKEL, on holding on to what she'd built while at the same time capitalizing on what she'd built: "When I did my original 'Skinnygirl' deal, I didn't really understand the difference between licensing and equity. All I knew when selling to Beam was that I didn't think they needed the name or the 'girl' logo in any other category besides alcohol, because alcohol was all they did. That was their only business, while I had all these other businesses I wanted to pursue, so it was a deal-breaker for me."

I didn't know Bethenny at the time, but I remember reading about that deal when it went down and thinking, *Damn!* It struck me then (and still!) as a pure power play on Bethenny's part, and from the outside looking in I thought it came about because Bethenny was holding all the best cards. But when you broke it down and looked at it from both sides, Bethenny's request wasn't really a power play at all. Yes, keeping the name was important to her—and yes, she was willing to walk away from the deal without it. But what she was asking for wasn't anything the Beam people seemed to require. That's how it goes in a negotiation when you don't *have* to do the deal: You can ask for the moon and expect to get it. And in this case, to hear Bethenny tell it, the *powershift* came about because it never occurred to Bethenny that what she was seeking was an unreasonable ask. All she knew was that this was what she wanted, and that this was what she believed she was entitled to, so she put it out there.

Ultimately, the deal helped Beam to create (and own!) an entirely new category in the spirits industry, which paid off for them in a big way, while Bethenny got approximately a hundred million dollars for just the spirits end of the business while holding on to the name and to the brand itself.

Today, even before Bethenny enters into a negotiation on a new deal she always has a clear idea in her head of the value she brings to the table and the value she expects to come her way in return. "I don't play games with numbers," she tells me. "If I know my value is five dollars, I'm going to ask for five dollars. I'm not going to pretend I really want ten dollars and then settle for five dollars." Her thinking when she embarks on a new partnership is that she's going to be working with this person or that group of people for years and years—that's been the case with her show with Bravo, and her books with Simon & Schuster. When you keep your partners like that, it's a good sign that you're delivering on your promise.

REMEMBER WHEN THE TABLES WERE TURNED

The reason I pay good and close attention to my *Shark Tank* partners is because I know what it's like to be in their position. It wasn't that long ago that I was the one hustling to make a deal with an established partner who could help me launch my fashion brand, so I try to honor that each time out, and pay it forward however I can.

Back when I was starting out, I was lucky to have my friends Norman and Bruce of Samsung's textile division as investor-partners, because they were looking out for us. Of course, they weren't my friends when they first threw in with us on the deal, but they became my friends over time because I appreciated their guidance. I liked that they had our backs. They understood what FUBU meant to me and my boys. I knew I could trust them because they gave me every reason to trust them. On the flip side, I knew these guys needed to put certain parameters in place to ensure they got a return on their investment, so we had to be mindful of that as well.

Pretty much every decision we made in the early going came down to the two of them giving us what we wanted as long as we could find a way to give them what they wanted. Don't think either side ever said as much, but we were each committed to the other in this way. One of the first times this came up was when I went to Bruce and Norman concerned that our goods were going to wind up at a discount store. When you're a young designer, you don't want to see your clothes hanging on a discount rack—unless of course that's what you're targeting in the first place. If it's not, it can be the kiss of death, in terms of the public's perception of your line.

As manufacturing partners, Norman and Bruce focused on and cared mostly about managing our inventory and only a little bit about the cachet or street cred that would come our way on the back of each sale. *Perception,* to them, was about being fiscally responsible. So we came up with a way to give me and my boys what we wanted while at the same time giving Norman and Bruce the assurances they needed to know we were maximizing revenue. Basically, they told us we could design whatever type of line we wanted, and that we would have 90 days or in some cases 120 days to push it through mid-tier channels like Macy's and Bloomingdale's. After that, we agreed that they would have the ability to sell to discounters, or find another way to get rid of the goods, because all that inventory would be taking up space in our warehouse—and you know, it costs money to make the clothes, money to store the clothes, money to ship the clothes, and money to take back returns.

This seemed like a fair compromise—and it even pushed me to think more responsibly about what we were designing. Under these terms, we couldn't just come up with a line we liked and hope for the best. We were accountable. So my front-and-center goal was to create a line that was maybe a little less *out there* while staying aligned with the FUBU brand.

In every deal, you want to keep both sides focused on a shared goal. This 90-to-120-day window we had at FUBU was a good way to accomplish that, because it reassured us that our clothes weren't about to wind up in the discount bin and at the same time it reassured our partners that we weren't looking to design a wild line that would just languish in our warehouse.

The best way to honor multiple agendas on a deal is to acknowledge them. What I've found over the years is that this doesn't always happen. People have a tendency to take care of their own business and leave it to others to fend for themselves, but if you want a deal to work all the way around you've got to look at it every which way.

Here I want to isolate just a few strategies for keeping the conversation moving along mutually beneficial lines.

Some other things you should pay attention to (which I created a corresponding exercise for at DaymondJohn .com/PowershiftExtras) when you get in on a deal:

1. Be clear about what you're looking to accomplish.

Communication is key in any partnership. If we didn't share our concerns about the perception of selling our clothes in these discount chains, Samsung wouldn't have come up with this strategy to give us the room we needed to do our thing.

2. Don't let either side settle.

I go into every deal thinking there ought to be a way to get both sides close to what they need. This doesn't mean I'm a pushover, or a little too eager to give away the store; I've learned over the years that there is al-most always a mutually beneficial solution to any im-passe, and that you'll usually find it as long as you're committed to looking for it.

3. Don't be afraid to give up something your partner really wants.

Understand that the *powershift* in the transaction might come by giving something away in a deal that lets the other party feel like they've gotten tremendous value. And know this: It doesn't make you weak when you bend on a deal point that doesn't serve you directly. Sometimes you win by losing, right? Only here, unless you're fundamentally changing the business, it's not really a loss if what you're giving up can get your partner more excited about doing a deal. In fact, you could make the argument that what strengthens the other guy's hand strengthens your hand as well.

4. Don't be afraid to ask for what you want.

Remember the great lesson of Bethenny Frankel's Skinnygirl ask. It didn't occur to her that the carve-out she sought outside the spirits industry was unprecedented in a deal of this type. It simply checked off a few extra boxes for her on the long wish list of what she wanted to see happen. Demonstrate that what the other person is able to gain is worth more than whatever it is they might be giving up. Play to their *want*. Show them how the deal will look (and how their situation stands to improve) if they get this one point in their favor. If it works out that you can benefit from this one point as well, that's great; if it doesn't, you'll have laid in a truckload of goodwill, good karma . . . all of that.

5. Create a *powershift* opportunity for one of your partners in the deal.

People appreciate it when you're looking out for them. Focus on the other person's problem and not on the solution you have possibly identified. Work together to fix what's broken and set it up so all the other moving pieces have a chance to fall into place.

6. Toss the scorecard.

Too often, the most important deal points are obscured in a negotiation, especially in a conversation serving many agendas. When there are too many moving parts in a deal, it's tough to keep score—so why not toss the scorecard and focus on one deal point at a time? It's always worked for me to pay good and close attention to the major levers of the deal and keep the concentration focused on those.

7. Call out your own weaknesses.

It always pays to be honest—and when you can be honest about yourself, it pays most of all. I'm not suggesting here that you need to put yourself down or go out of your way to appear self-deprecating, but if you're asked to perform a task that's a little above your pay grade or just outside your wheelhouse, you should say so. Better to be clear at the outset than to leave room for surprises.

8. Don't let negative energy get in the way of a deal.

A lot of times when I'm in a negotiation, people have a fixed idea how things might go. They create certain narratives in their head. They feed themselves these self-defeating lines about how I must have some sort of advantage because I'm a professional negotiator, a serial entrepreneur, or whatever, but I try to defuse or deflect that type of thinking at every chance. I'll say something like "I know I'm on a show all about negotiating, but the truth is I like to approach every deal like it's the first deal I've ever done." When you approach these concerns in this way, you help to create an environment where you're encouraging open and honest conversation. Hopefully, the person you're negotiating with will become more comfortable, and together you'll be able to identify the obstacles and figure a way past them. If you're still sensing negative energy, don't take offense. It isn't personal. They're just trying to win the game.

POWER FACT Did you know that offering even a tiny unsolicited favor can improve your chances at getting to a win–win situation? Researchers at Santa Clara University found that people were more likely to comply with a request when they were given a favor at the time of asking—even if they did not think that the person making the request would ever find out if they completed it or not. Adding in minor "favors" to your end of the deal (even something as simple as agreeing to meet for lunch once a quarter to discuss how the deal has benefited each company) can actually motivate the opposite party to throw in a favor for you as well, improving the outcome for everyone.

PART III

RELATIONSHIPS
Make a Connection Last

The third gear you'll need to tap as you pivot into something new is a lifetime of meaningful relationships. The idea here is to keep a collection going, because these relationships are hard to come by. It's my version of that old line about treating people well on the way up because you never know who you'll meet on the way down—only we're not out to hit the down button on this elevator. No, we're out to climb ever higher, but we'll need to call on some of the people who've helped us along the way to help us hit our next target . . . and the one after that . . . and the one after that. Find a way to nurture every positive relationship you've developed in your life and career. These are the connections you'll need to help get you where you want to go.

Chapter 11

UNDERSTAND THAT PEOPLE ARE PEOPLE (JUST LIKE YOU)

One of the things that was hardest for me to figure out as a young entrepreneur was that I wasn't the only one trying to move the needle and step into my future. Every vendor, every customer, every "influencer" I was trying to get into one of our shirts . . . they were all busy trying to make their own *powershifts.* The thing is, I tended to think about other people in terms of what they could do for me, instead of what I could do for them—or even better, what we could do for each other.

Big mistake.

What I came to realize was that when you have your head down and you're completely focused on the road ahead is precisely the time you need to keep your head up and your eyes open. It's like how you're not supposed to text while you're driving: **If you're only thinking about what you want to say or what impacts you directly, you'll never see or appreciate or be in any kind of position to react to everything that's happening all around you.** You can't build a lasting relationship with your vendors and customers if you're only thinking about your own thing.

Doesn't matter what business or relationship you're in— the way you move forward is with and through and alongside other people.

So go ahead and keep doing your thing, but make room for the idea that everyone else is out doing *their* thing as well.

It's human nature to forget the human nature of our interactions. What do I mean by that? Well, we tend to take one another for granted, and I've found that this is especially true when we're talking about our business relationships. **We're taught to look at outcomes, when we should really be paying attention to the people who help us achieve those outcomes.**

Think about it: When you're looking to get something out of an interaction with another person, it's easy to forget that there's a human being on the other side of the table. There was a time in my life when I was as guilty of this as anyone, until I was finally made to realize that every person I do business with, every person I associate with away from work, is cut the same as me.

UNDERSTAND THAT PEOPLE ARE PEOPLE (JUST LIKE YOU)

We're all the same, in the end. We get up each morning with our own goals for the day, a punch list of what we want to accomplish, a warning list of what we want to avoid, and it just might be that *my* goals are standing in the way of the other person's goals from time to time. Or maybe it happens that my goals can be of service. Either way, it's something I've learned to pay attention to, so one of the things I try to do when I'm dealing with someone is to separate out all the facts and figures and deal points and try to look at whatever's under discussion from the other person's perspective.

That's why, when Bethenny Frankel sits in on the *Shark Tank* panel she tries to think about what the entrepreneurs *want* out of the deal and weighs it alongside what they *ask* in a deal. "You don't want to squeeze these young entrepreneurs," she tells me. "So I listen to what they're saying and remind myself to think of them as my equal. We're all just people, right?"

Here I think it pays to remember that the most successful pitches on *Shark Tank* come from entrepreneurs who take the time to figure out what makes us Sharks tick as individuals. For example, Robert believes that emotion in business can be an asset, as producer Clay Newbill pointed out to me when I interviewed him for this book. And one of the things I've noticed is that Robert likes to feel like a rock star with his investments—a savior who comes in on his white horse and saves the day. If you're able to play into that with a pitch, you've got a better shot of getting some buy-in.

Mark, for his part, is always looking for ways to create synergy with the Dallas Mavericks, or to leverage his contacts with other team owners and major venues across the country. With me, regular viewers of the show know that I'm a sucker for any deal with a charitable component to it. For example, they know that I'm on the board of the Petco Foundation, which is devoted to animal welfare work across the country, and various other organizations that put good back into their communities, so any pitch that speaks into this space has a good chance of getting my attention.

How can I show my appreciation for someone else's contribution?

Is there anything more I can get into a deal that will make a meaningful difference for the other person, without changing my own position in a material way?

What follow-through do I need to put in place to ensure that I'm delivering on my promises?

If you're able to ask yourself these kinds of questions, and put proactive answers into play, you'll be able to at least start building the kind of lasting relationships that will serve you going forward.

BREAK THE BOX

Okay, so these days I try to move about with my head up and my eyes open, but back in the day I didn't have the maturity to see the world in this way. In fact, when things were on blast with FUBU, I could be pretty arrogant at times, maybe even a little selfish, and I've got a story to illustrate. We were so hot back then, it went to our heads. The way we sold our goods to retailers in those days was in a kind of pre-pack. We had a certain number of smalls, a certain number of mediums, a certain number of larges and extra-larges. Or with pants, a certain number of thirty-four waists, a certain number of thirty-sixes, thirty-eights . . . whatever. Let's say there were a dozen jeans in the box and the wholesale cost to the retailer was six hundred dollars, but then we'd hear back that their customer base ran on the large side and they couldn't really move those thirty-twos or thirty-fours. Or maybe it worked out that the situation was reversed—they couldn't sell the bigger sizes—so they'd reach out to us and see if we could maybe help them out.

We called it "breaking the box," when we'd dip into these pre-packs and allow a retailer to customize an order—and like a lot of designers, this wasn't something we wanted to do. It took time, and it was a little bit of a hassle—and when you're selling through your inventory like crazy and making a bunch of money, **the rookie move is to value the hustle over the hassle.** At first, it felt to us like there was no reason even to have this conversation. Of course, I know now that this was not at all the case, but at the time our clothes were so hot, we were pretty arrogant and pigheaded. We weren't about to get involved with these types of requests, because they weren't worth our time. Someone would call and say, "Can you work with me on this?" And we'd be like, "No way." That was our stupid thinking.

As a general rule of thumb, when one of your partners or someone you hope to do repeat business with asks you if you can work with them to make some kind of adjustment to your agreement, you should at least take the time to listen. It might be that what they need from you doesn't make sense or is against your interests, but it could just as easily be a no-cost accommodation on your part—so consider the ask. Turn it down if it doesn't make sense, but give the other person the respect of a full and fair hearing before you do.

In the moment, we were able to get away with our arrogant, pigheaded approach, because these stores needed us more than we needed them. That's a dangerous combo when you're just starting out, because that early success tricks you into thinking business will always be this good. And for a while, it was: Customers were coming in, asking for FUBU, so these retailers had no choice but to stock our products, even if they had to eat the cost of these few items they could never sell. But after a while, the situation flipped. We started to lose some of our shine, and once our clothes weren't in such high demand, these store owners were no longer on our side.

Now, for the major retailers and department stores, it played out a little differently. We knew enough to compromise with them on this, because they represented such a big part of our business. Even if we had to take back a couple million dollars' worth of clothes on a twenty-million-dollar order, it made sense. But we didn't show the same kind of love to the little guys, because I couldn't see any good reason to do so at the time, and you better believe that would come back to bite us. Because we were too lazy or too cocky or too full of ourselves to break the box and service these retailers in the right way, it ended up costing us in the long run. Instead of getting these guys in our corner and trying to work hard for us because we were working hard for them, we forced them to find a way to cover the cost of whatever they couldn't sell. In this case, that meant we'd left them no choice but to start discounting our gear. When that happens, as I mentioned earlier, it starts to corrode the brand—customers begin to write you off as old news and start to look for the next "hot" brand. You know how that goes, right? You walk into a store and you see a rack of a couple hundred pairs of FUBU jeans selling for dirt-cheap, so you start to think there must be something wrong with them.

Clearly, we could have figured out some other way to help them out. We could have sold a box of just one size, or taken the time to break up our pre-packs and deliver orders that served the needs of those customers. But instead we took advantage of the position we were in and failed to consider the human side of the equation. We didn't stop to think that these smaller retailers were usually family-owned, mom-and-pop type businesses—aspiring entrepreneurs, just like us. We didn't take the time to consider that these were relationships we needed to nurture, and keep strong, if we wanted to keep the *brand* strong over the long haul.

And out of that short-sightedness, we forced their hand. Basically, we were lazy. We didn't show these people the love or appreciation they deserved, and because of that they didn't go out of their way for us, either. And worse, our competitors were probably out there making these accommodations—because, really, it was no big deal—so we were doubly screwed. I mean, why would these people keep doing business with us if we were so inflexible, if they could just go across the street and buy similar goods from another designer who was willing to cater to address their concerns?

We'd left them no choice.

My point here is that relationships are all-important. Yeah, go ahead and make a good deal for yourself, but don't let your head get so big that you stop caring about the people who helped get you to where you are. Here we could have easily addressed some of these concerns with just a little bit of extra effort and attention, but we were more focused on making the sale than on supporting the needs of our partners. And in the end, that cost us their business and their loyalty.

"TAKE ADVANTAGE OF TONIGHT"

I'm betting some readers will recognize the line in this header. It's from a Pitbull song called "Give Me Every-thing," featuring Ne-Yo, Afrojack, and Nayer, and it gets a mention here because it fits with this theme.

When the two of us were swapping *powershift* stories, Pit

told me about the time he was in Saint-Tropez, and he was stopped on his way out of a club by a girl who wanted to take a picture of him. Nothing new here, right? Except for some reason, the security guys at the club tried to chase her away. The whole time, Pit was waving her back to him, wanting to help her out. One thing about my friend Pit— he's generous with his fans. He makes time for them, because he appreciates the time they've made in their lives for him. With him, it cuts both ways, so he's always extending himself, making himself available in ways that most artists are not.

So after a little back-and-forth, this fan came up and got her picture, and after that the two of them got to talking. It was kind of a frantic scene, but when the girl asked him to put her in touch with someone she thought could maybe help her out on a project, Pit gave her his number. Wasn't something he typically did, but he figured, Why not? And that was that, for the next little while. A couple weeks later, the girl hit him up, and it turned out she was a princess from Dubai—an actual, legit princess, like something out of a fairy tale.

That's why he went and wrote that song:

"Take advantage of tonight, 'cause tomorrow I'm off to Dubai to perform for a princess."

It turned out to be his first number one hit—one of his biggest songs to date—and it came on the back of this simple kindness.

"If it wasn't for the fact that I opened up to this girl," he says, "that song never would have happened. It changed my life, that song. And it's just, you know, because I was humble enough to say to these guys, 'Don't worry about it.' Because I took the time to talk to her, and she was so appreciative, and it opened up this connection."

Look, I'm not suggesting here that if you live in the public eye you should be dropping that velvet rope and giving your number to anyone and everyone, but clearly Pit saw something in this girl, in the way she carried herself, that told him to let his guard down here. He didn't just see her as a fan wanting to get close to him. He saw her as a person, just like him, and he could sense she had something important to share.

Can you think of a time in your life when you dropped your defenses and connected with someone you might have otherwise overlooked? Go over that list and see how many times you won when you didn't overlook something. Take inventory. Think back to those times when you made a concession on a deal. Did it reward you in some way? Was there some connection that came back to you on the bounce?

REMEMBER THE ONE ABOUT THE TERMITE WHO WALKED INTO A BAR?

Here's another great example of someone going out of his way to make a human connection with a prospective partner—and this time, *I* was the one on the receiving end of a generous turn.

Remember my digital marketing partner Billy Gene Shaw? He's the savvy tech guru I introduced you to earlier who's helped to drive traffic to Daymond on Demand, my online educational platforms through Facebook ads and other social media. Well, the first time I met Billy, he went out of his way to make the kind of first impression that would help him begin to make a lasting one. Even though he knew he had the goods to impress me with his knowledge of digital media in its own right, he really put some time and thought into coming up with a couple ways to make an impressive personal pitch.

Then he decided to go himself one better.

He'd learned I had a thing for "dad jokes"—you know, those corny, cringe-worthy one-liners that are so bad they're good.

Like,

> "Dad, did you get a haircut?"
> "No, I got them all cut."

Or,

> "What do you call a fish with no eyes?"
> "A fsssh."

Or just one more . . . for now:

> "What's E.T. short for?"
> "Because he's only got little legs."

I'm sorry, but I have a weakness for these jokes, and around the time Billy and I were due to meet I'd given a couple interviews in which I talked about my obsession for this weird little art form. I was even in the habit of posting some of my favorites on Instagram and Twitter, and the people who followed me kept hitting me back with some dad jokes of their own.

So what did Billy do? He went out and got me a book of hundreds of dad jokes, and then he took the time to highlight some of *his* favorites, and make little notes in the margins. It was such a sweetly personal gesture that it couldn't help but hit home in a special way—and out of that, the two of us became friends, over this one goofy bond. This is a perfect example of what I mean when I talk about opening a file on someone. Now, whenever I think of Billy, I think of the way he went out of his way here, and the common ground we share over these dad jokes—same way I used to think of that guy with the cartoonish double takes in my Scooby-Doo file. It's a way to keep everything straight in my mind, and allows me to quickly access the meaningful points of connection I've developed with hundreds (even thousands!) of people over the years.

All of which begs the question: Did *you* hear the one about the termite who walked into a bar? He asked, "Is the bar*tender* here?"

(Groan.)

Look, there are all kinds of ways to make and maintain these special bonds with the people you work with, and it doesn't always have to pay immediate dividends (or involve corny jokes). Me, I like to fish, so it follows that I like to go fishing with my business partners. You can tell a lot about people by the way they wait for a bite, but it's also a great way to get to know somebody away from the heat and haste of a busy workday. There's nothing like powering down your phones and stepping into a picture-postcard type environment for getting to know someone as they really are.

What are some of your favorite go-to activities that might allow you to connect with a partner or colleague in a way that shows a side of yourself that might further your business relationship?

What are some ways you can relate what you do away from work to the work at hand?

If others look to relate to you in the same way, are you prepared to respond?

Yeah, yeah, yeah . . . Dad jokes aren't everyone's thing—I *get* that. But spend some time thinking of ways to bond with people, to grow your professional relationships away from the workplace, and you'll see the benefits over time. And while you're at it, here are a few additional points to keep in mind:

1. Accept that it is better to give than to receive.

It's always better to extend a hand than to hold your hand out. That's one of the reasons I get excited about mentoring young entrepreneurs. I'm not looking to get anything back out of the deal, other than the feel-good elements that come from seeing someone find the success they deserve. But at the same time, I've also come to believe that if you put good things out into the world, good things will come back to you on the bounce.

2. Know that there is never a good time to stop working in service of your reputation.

This is especially true if you live in the light of celebrity. When you've got a platform, there will always be haters looking to knock you off it, so don't give them any ammunition. Live your life as if the whole world is watching, 24/7.

3. Be slow to judge and quick to forgive.

Actually, don't judge at all. Really. You never know when the tables might turn and you'll be the one hoping others can find a way to forgive, excuse, or look past one of your screwups. In the *karma's a bitch* department, you can expect to get back the good *and* the bad you put out into the world, so be inclined to cut other people some slack.

4. Establish trust.

In his excellent book on the science of creating a winning corporate environment, *Trust Factor,* the economist Paul J. Zak writes about the power of building and maintaining trust in your professional relationships. According to Zak, when someone trusts you, you're inclined to trust them—not *just* because you're good people who have each other's backs but because there's actually a triggering jolt to the brain of a hormone called oxytocin that makes us want to reciprocate.

5. Give it time.

One of the biggest mistakes an individual can make in trying to salvage a reputation is to come at it too soon. Sometimes it helps to put some distance between a screwup and a repair job. Put an immediate end to whatever's gotten you into hot water in the first place, but then step back and let things cool a little before trying to set things right.

POWER FACT Let your people know their voices are being heard. According to a Salesforce survey, your people are 4.6 times more likely to work their butts off for you and to perform at their best if they feel their opinions are valued. So let them know you're listening.

Chapter 12

BRING VALUE WITHOUT EXPECTING ANYTHING IN RETURN

"WORK LIKE THERE IS SOMEONE WORKING TWENTY-FOUR HOURS A DAY TO TAKE IT AWAY FROM YOU."

That's a line from Mark Cuban, and I put it out here to set up this next bunch of pages, where I want to look at the choices we make as we look to add value to every interaction and transaction—even when it might not be clear to us that we're getting any kind of return on our investment.

By the way, every time I come across Mark's line I want to amend it to say, "Work like there is someone working twenty-four hours a day to make a better impression than you." That's because success is about the extra efforts you put into a deal . . . or a project . . . or an opportunity. Those extra efforts can be tough to define, and they're especially tough to define when we're our own boss, but they make all the difference.

One thing I've learned over the years is that the efforts we put into our work or our relationships are directly related to the size and scope of our commitments. Put another way, once we figure out where it is we'd like to be, that's when we work like crazy to get there as quickly as possible. The tough part, for those of us who have *lots of places* we'd like to be, is knowing where to focus the bulk of our efforts. Like a lot of people, I look at my daily calendar and start to think I'm spreading myself thin. My commitments are off the charts. There's always a deadline or a meeting or a pile of emails waiting for my attention. I'm constantly moving, doing, dealing . . . really, it can get to where I sometimes feel like I'm being kept from the things in life that matter to me most. This hit me most of all after I got my cancer diagnosis a couple years back, when I was pushed to think about why I was here on this earth and what I mean to leave behind.

Another thing I've learned: No one is sitting on his deathbed saying, "Jeez, I wish I'd spent more time at the office."

But what *does* tend to come up as we breathe our last is the way we've honored the relationships in our lives— family, friends, colleagues, mentors, mentees. While I'm still alive and kicking, the way I try to honor these good people is by beating their expectations, and making those extra efforts in service of *their* goals as well as mine, and to do all of this without a thought about what's in it for me.

My take: I'm here, doing what I'm doing, because I busted my butt to build my business and make my name. Ten, twenty years from now, I'll be doing what I'm doing because I busted my butt today. Now, the main reason I bust my butt is because that's how I'm wired. I'm determined to get results—and sometimes it means that in order to get results I've got to outhustle everyone else. But there's another reason that sits alongside this first one: I never want to let anybody down. After all, **I'm not working just for myself—I'm working for everyone else in my orbit.**

You know how one of the things you're supposed to do when you go camping is leave your campsite in better shape than you found it? Meaning, we're not only supposed to pick up after ourselves, we're also taught to clean up after the people who made camp before us. Maybe they left some nasty cooking utensils in the fire pit, or maybe they dropped a couple empty water bottles on the perimeter of the campsite. Whatever it is, it's on you to set things right, even though you get nothing out of it. That's kind of what we're after here, the idea of putting in more than you take out, even if you get nothing out of it other than the knowledge that you're doing the right thing.

We should be thinking along these same lines when it comes to business, or to making our relationships work, because our extra efforts will come to define us—*especially* the extra efforts we make when there's nothing in it for us.

That's why I'm always giving away free content to my followers online—mostly because I'm so totally grateful for their support. Of course, a cynic would say that when I make the first hour of one of my online courses available at no cost to my fans, or the first chapter of this book, it's simply a marketing play—you know, a come-on meant to entice people into buying the full package. I can see that, I guess. That's why I stuck that *mostly* qualifier in that statement above. But what's *really* driving me when I give away content in this way is the satisfaction that comes from knowing I might have turned someone on to a new approach, or to a strategy that just might take them from where they are to where they want to be . . . and I certainly don't need to be making paper off *that*. It doesn't matter to me if they sign on and subscribe or buy or whatever—I've been at this long enough to know there'll be enough customers to sign on for the full ride. The idea, always, is to overdeliver—and in the goes-without-saying department, you obviously want to make sure that what you're overdelivering is first-rate. I mean, if what you're putting out there is horrible, it doesn't matter if you're giving it away or selling it at a steep discount . . . nobody's gonna want it.

This last bit about giving with no expectation of return is key, because a lot of times when people overdeliver on a project or a promise, they do it with the expectation that it will pay dividends for them in the future. A lot of times, it will—only here I want to stress that **our focus should be not on the dividends but on the investment.**

Going back to the first side hustles I threw together as a

kid—fixing up old cars, say—I found that I worked double time, double hard when I had a partner. Over the years, I've looked for partners who are cut the same way. If this is what drives me and keeps me honest, I can only assume that it's also driving my partners and keeping *them* honest. And keep in mind, I'm not *just* looking out for my partners when I deliver on a promise. I'm also looking out for the people on the other side of the table, making sure that whatever good deal I'm negotiating for myself is also a good deal for them.

If that sounds like a line . . . well, you've never sat across from me on a deal. Don't get me wrong. I'm not looking to give away the store, or cost myself an opportunity, but I'm always looking for ways to extend myself or put a little extra something into my efforts, whether or not there's any direct benefit to me.

And if *that* sounds like a line . . . well, check it out: Do you know how people are always saying life is too short for this or that? *Life is too short for me to be screwing people over. Life is too short for my success to come at someone else's expense. Life is too short for me to be out there cutting corners.* I hear those kinds of comments and I get to thinking they're upside down—or missing the point. **It's not *just* because life is too short that we should do right by the people we do business with; it's because the world is too damn small.** What goes around comes around, right? That's one of the reasons I go out of my way to treat people fairly, even generously, because you never know when your paths will cross again.

Just think of the power that comes from flipping that

switch and going out of your way to do someone a solid, so that instead of dreading the day when you run into that person you find yourself looking forward to it . . . *counting on it,* even. Don't know about you but I'd much rather build a network of onetime colleagues or deal partners who are happy with the way things turned out for them after meeting me than a bunch of people who have more neutral feelings about our repeat business.

Here's another quote to help me make my point—a line I often see on banners hanging in a school auditorium or gymnasium when I'm invited to talk to students about how to rise and grind and make a name for themselves in business: **"The true test of a man's character is what he does when no one is watching."**

That's a line from legendary UCLA basketball coach John Wooden, who certainly knew a thing or two about working tirelessly and thanklessly and selflessly in pursuit of excellence.

Some of the people you've met in these pages answer this test of character with a call to charity. They donate their time and money to projects and causes that promise them nothing in return . . . *except* for the satisfaction of knowing they're helping to repair the world, in their own way. It's the *powershift* version of leaving your campsite in better shape than you found it.

Check it out:

- Pitbull has dedicated himself to helping the Latino community and closing the poverty gap by opening up a network of tuition-free charter schools for middle school and high school students. He calls his schools SLAM!, for "Sports Leadership and Management," and as I write this they're operating in Las Vegas, Atlanta, and Miami's Little Havana neighborhood, where Pit grew up. "I feel like the system isn't built to help you," he tells me of his extra efforts here. "I feel like a lot of these kids can do so much more than what we expect of them, if we just let them know we believe in them. You let them know, Yo, this is what's possible. I tell them, If I can do it, you can do it, and you can do it bigger, better, badder, stronger."

• Lindsey Vonn started the Lindsey Vonn Foundation as a way to empower young girls and offer them the kind of role modeling and mentoring they might not get at school or at home. She's developed a weekend-long curriculum to teach strategies and inner-strength-building exercises designed to foster a sense of independence and community—an extension of the *don't quit* mindset that defined her as a skier, coming back from a string of injuries. Right now, she offers these camps free of charge to girls in New York, Los Angeles, and Las Vegas, and she's hoping to add more cities in the future. She says, "My mission is to empower and inspire the next generation to follow their dreams." Her inspiration came from a meeting she had at nine years old, when she had the chance to visit with her idol, the Olympic gold medalist Picabo Street. "That one meeting changed my life and it lasted just five minutes," she says. "Just think of the impact we can make if I can get to work with these girls for two whole days and get them thinking they can do just about anything."

• David Heath, of Bombas, recognizes the importance that mentorship has played in his own career, so he makes time to mentor others. "I will always carve out some time in my calendar, despite how busy I've gotten," he says. "Most of the time, it's with someone who hasn't even launched yet. You know, it's super, super early days, but I make the time because people once made the time for me, and the hope here is that someday this person will be in a position to pay it forward and make the same kind of time for someone else."

So tell me, what are *you* doing when no one else is watching?

DO THE MATH

Believe me, I've done my share of deals that lean in my favor. And yes, I'm always out to negotiate from strength. But here's the truth: I'd much prefer to deal from strength to strength than from strength to weakness, because **when you give as good as you get you're also seeding your future.**

Whatever the deal is, whatever's at stake in the near term, I tell myself I'm working in service of the next deal, and the one after that. I'm working for the long term.

It rubs me the wrong way when people step into a transaction thinking only about what's in it for them, because I've found over the years that the universe has a way of rewarding you if you're committed to working hard and adding value. So instead of asking "What's in it for me?" when you consider a deal, you should be asking "What can I add?"

In the end, it's what you *put into* an enterprise that drives its success.

When we commit ourselves to *adding* value instead of *extracting* it, we commit to making the kind of lasting impression with our partners that will serve the entire operation in the future. **By growing relationships from a place of service, you will not only make yourself a more desirable partner or collaborator, but also establish a foundation of trust and goodwill you'll be able to draw on if you're ever in need of a good turn.**

Basically, my rule of thumb is to add three times the value I extract from any relationship before asking for something in return. That doesn't mean I'm sitting there with a calculator, trying to measure or quantify my extra efforts, but I am paying good and close attention to the way we balance the scales.

Anyway, the math isn't hard:

- I'll work through dinner three times before asking someone on my staff to do the same.

- I'll share a friend's tweet or post three times before asking him or her to share one of mine.

- I'll offer to help someone move or drive them to the airport or take care of their dog three times before calling on them to extend a similar kindness.

You get the idea.

My thing is to overdeliver whenever I can. It reminds me of those "Wait, wait . . . there's more!" ads you always used to see on late-night television. (They're still out there, matter of fact!) One of the reasons that line has been so effective as an advertising or marketing strategy is that it plays on people's desire to feel like they're getting more value, so I figure that if it works when you're selling Ginsu knives or Pocket Fishermen or whatever the case may be, it should also work when you're selling yourself. Go out of your way to let people know they're getting a good deal when they decide to work with you, or hire you, or spend any kind of meaningful time with you. And then, just when they start to thinking you're really going above and beyond, go ahead and give 'em a little extra.

Of course, in everything I do, everything I sell, I try to make sure there's a money-back-guarantee component to the transaction. In my "Daymond on Demand" courses, I want to make sure my customers are completely satisfied—same goes for audiences at my lectures and keynotes. Whenever people deal with me, in any capacity, I want them to be happy with the exchange, and to look back on it as a positive experience. This is important to me—it's the human element at the heart of those late-night infomercials I just talked about, because people always want to feel like they're getting value . . . like they're getting just a little bit more than everybody else, even. And yet you might be surprised to learn that less than ten percent of infomercials are actually successful—meaning they end up making money for the producer or marketer. This is key, because, end of the day, the product is king. If what you're selling doesn't match up with the extraordinary claims you're making in order to sell it . . . well, then you're nowhere, baby.

It's important to try to measure the success of each relationship by its long-term impact, and not on any short-term benefits that may come your way as a result. So do yourself a favor and resist the idea of engaging only with people who can give you something in return. The better move—the *powershift* move—is to nurture long-term connections that will prove mutually beneficial over time.

Don't know about you, but one of my pet peeves is dealing with people who operate from a place of laziness or phoniness—really, there's nothing worse than having to make room in your life for someone who's always looking for the easy way around. We all know the type, right? They'll say anything to get themselves in the door or to close a deal, but their promises are empty. You deal with them once and never again. Or maybe you only hear from them when they need something, because they live and work on a one-way street. And so, whatever you do, *don't be that person!* Got to admit, I can be quick to write people off if they don't deliver for me. The way I look at it is, if you can't be a good friend to yourself, you can't be a good friend to me. Yeah, I'll give someone the benefit of the doubt, but I'm not out there dishing out chance after chance, because that just doesn't serve anyone in the end. Try to remember that the most important part of building, growing, and sustaining a constructive relationship is to put out the highest level of authenticity and integrity through-out each part of the process. Your relationships are your greatest source of capital. Invest in them meaningfully and honestly, and they will grow. Squander them on false ex-pectations or selfish pursuits and you'll soon find yourself on your own.

Another way to put it: Be good to your word and your word will be good to you.

MEET (AND EXCEED) EXPECTATIONS

Honoring your commitments and overdelivering on your promises is important for everyone, and it's espe-cially important in the world of entrepreneurs and free-lancers, where you're constantly chasing your next gig, your next paycheck. When you work for yourself, it's easy to forget the importance of building a lasting, two-way relationship because the tendency is to think in one-and-done terms.

It used to be that this was an isolated concern, because the majority of American workers were in an office somewhere, or on some assembly line, locked into the routine that comes with a full-time job. That's changed dramatically in our digital age: **The nine-to-five model is about as relevant to today's workplace as the rotary phone.** More and more, people are working from home, making a living as freelancers or gig workers in fields ranging from consulting, to programming, to graphic design. I often sit down with the big companies to teach their executives and employees how to address this changing landscape and to act like "intrapreneurs"—people who think like entrepreneurs within a big company. People are working odd hours more and more. And people are switching jobs more and more, too. According to a January 2018 report from the Bureau of Labor Statistics, the average person changes jobs ten to fifteen times during their career, and many workers spend five years or less in every job. The workday itself doesn't really have a clock on it anymore—meaning, productivity can happen whenever or wherever we find a pocket of time to send a text or answer an email or sit in on a videoconference call.

Also, I recently read a CNBC report that said the majority of American workers will be contract workers by 2027. It's possible to look at this stat as an encouraging sign and a discouraging sign at the same time. Yeah, it might be an alarming indicator of the trend to cut costs by eliminating or reducing full-time payroll, but at the same time it signals that more and more workers will be able to call their own shots each time they take on a new position or assignment. It's easy to look at this evolution in our traditional work model and start to feel like the pressures of career are never-ending and overwhelming; that technology has made it just about impossible to step away from the office and power down. I get that. In a lot of ways, that's the thinking behind that Mark Cuban quote I used to open the chapter, but I take a different view. I take it as a giant positive, that there are all these different ways for us to call our own shots and add value in each and every transaction. So the message here, for me, is that **there is great power in the new digital workplace.** There's the power to set our own hours, determine our own workloads, drive our own projects. It's a different take on the *speed of determination* idea we talked about earlier: We set our own pace, together with our clients or whoever's signing our checks.

As we bounce around from job to job, or gig to gig, it's especially important to strengthen our relationships with customers and clients, with movers and shakers in our industry, and with our own colleagues—whether they work at the next desk or clear across the country. After all, these relationships are portable. They attach to us in a fundamental way. Even when we switch jobs, we're able to call on the support network we've built to make that switch possible, so the next time you pack up your desk to hit up a new opportunity remember to take those relationships with you. Take the time to let people know you're moving on and that you plan to call on them in the future—letting them know that you're hoping to keep hearing from them as well.

And let's remember that as our workdays become more fluid than ever before, it doesn't mean we should be looking for ways to run and hide from our obligations. Many of us no longer report to any one boss, or to any one office, so it's possible there are times when nobody *really* knows what we're doing from one day to the next, but I see that as a time to double down and grind harder and smarter to make doubly sure that the people who've hired you know they're getting their money's worth.

At The Shark Group, for example, we've found that it makes a whole lot of sense to hire "virtual assistants" to fill certain roles for us, over certain stretches, and assign them to specific projects—usually working with them on a month-to-month basis, for a set amount of hours each week.

Lately, this setup has been working out so well for us (and hopefully, for the assistants who sign on to work with us!) that we recently hired a full-time digital manager to work with us remotely, all the way from Ohio. Her name is Crystal Volinchak, and I'm betting some readers will be able to see a little something of themselves in Crystal's story. Previously, Crystal was working at Youngstown State University, for the Ohio Small Business Development Center. She's got an MBA, and she studied psychology as an undergrad, so she's certainly got the educational chops to make her an asset to any organization, and here she was putting her skills to use helping local entrepreneurs start or grow their businesses. While she was punching the clock on this straight-up nine-to-five job, she never imagined herself working outside a conventional office environment. The traditional job was what she knew. Then she got pregnant and just assumed she'd come back to work following her maternity leave—because this, too, was what she knew. But that's not exactly how things worked out. It ended up, she had a difficult pregnancy, was even put on bed rest for a stretch. Her son Primo was born a month and a half early, so he had to spend a bunch of time in the NICU, and once Crystal and her husband got the all-clear to take him home the baby still needed all kinds of extra care.

On top of all that, there was a change in policy at the university that made it so that employees like Crystal couldn't return to work on a part-time basis, which had been her plan for until she could sort out her daycare options. So right away she started thinking of ways she could maybe do the same type of work out of her own home, as a kind of independent contractor. Crystal's main concern with this type of work was struggling to find valid, reputable jobs. She knew there are all sorts of scams she might come across, so she turned to the virtual solutions company BELAY. If you're not familiar with the company, it acts as an intermediary that vets both virtual workers and online job opportunities to match up the best pairs and ensure that all of the jobs and virtual assistants are valid. I know virtual assistant might sound like something from the future involving AI and robotics, but all it means is that you're working remotely.

Crystal was like a lot of people I talk to looking to transition into the life of the self-employed, working on a self-directed schedule—she didn't trust that she could make it work on a full-time basis and decided she needed a bit of a safety net. So what did she do? She doubled up on her workload, adding her freelance work to her full-time job at the university, logging as much as eighty hours some weeks.

That's the kind of foundation you need to build before you make the kind of *powershift* Crystal had in mind. She took the time to make an impression and establish the kind of reputation that would get her hired. Then she made herself invaluable in a way that allowed her to negotiate the best deal for herself. And finally, she worked hard to over-deliver on each job she was able to land, so that she was in the strongest possible position to land the next one.

One of the best ways to build strong working relationships—especially when you work remotely—is simply to become as indispensable as possible. With this in mind, Crystal pays special attention to her delivery schedule. She's careful not to commit to a deadline unless she is absolutely certain she'll be able to meet it. Very often, she'll suggest a more relaxed time line for turning around a project, to give herself a cushion in case the other people she'll be collaborating with are unable to make themselves fully available in a timely manner. If it works out that she's able to beat her targeted deadline, that's great for all concerned. If others are dragging their feet and slow to complete their assigned tasks, she'll still be able to rally the troops in time to hit her due date.

Crystal also understands the importance of maintaining a consistent "presence" around the office. What I've noticed from my team is that you should set up regular meetings with your team, on a platform like Zoom or Skype if possible, and let the people you're working for know if you're going to be unavailable to them over a certain period. That's why Crystal makes it a special point to send her clients a weekly update, detailing the progress she's made on each project and outlining next steps. "It's a great way to remind the people you're working for of the value you're bringing to their business," she explains, "because when you're working remotely it's not like they can walk by your desk and see what you're doing every day.

"If I'm going on vacation," she continues, "I'll give my clients as much notice as possible. I'll give them a little extra time the week before I leave, and a little extra time when I get back. We'll move our targets around, so we can find a way to hit them together. I'll even get on the phone with them to work through a problem, if something comes up while I'm away. Ideally, it works out that they don't even know I'm gone, so even though the vacation might cost me in terms of my billable hours, it shouldn't cost me anything in terms of my accountability. I'm still completely there for them."

A lot of times, it works out that Crystal finds herself answering emails or returning phone calls on her days off, because she's made herself so invaluable while she's on the clock that she can't fully step away from the work when she's *off* the clock—a textbook example of overdelivering on a promise without expecting anything back.

Of course, Crystal would tell you that this is probably not the best long-term strategy for creating a healthy work–life balance, but she recognizes that a certain amount of *grind* is necessary as she's working to make a name for herself as a freelancer. In the meantime, she's found a way to build relationships in this space because she's learned to **deliver as much as she possibly can instead of as little as she can get away with.**

It's kind of like how when I was working at Red Lobster while I was trying to get FUBU off the ground, I made it a special point to sell the add-ons management was always pushing on customers. I resisted the idea at first, but eventually I sucked it up and did it anyway because it was important to management—and because I knew that my bosses at the restaurant were being judged by my performance. *Their* bosses would be on them if I didn't try to get people to order a second round of drinks or an appetizer or dessert. I came to see that I wasn't *just* doing my job but was making their lives easier at the same time, and as a bonus I made myself more and more invaluable, because I was helping them achieve their objectives. Plus, it didn't suck that I made a bunch of extra money in tips as a result!

Let's face it, we all have people in our lives who are looking to coast, or get by with a minimal effort, but if we think about the people we know who've enjoyed massive success we tend to see that they're the ones who over-deliver, again and again.

Just how do you put yourself in that kind of position?

1. Move with integrity.

Make doubly sure that every project, every meeting, every interaction is handled with absolute profession-alism. Think of every opportunity as your first and last and best opportunity to make a lasting impression.

2. Create alliances that are transformative, not transactional.

Even if there's a part of you thinking there ought to be some sort of immediate benefit to each and every interaction, condition yourself to think long-term. Resist the urge to keep score, or to engage only in projects that seem to offer instant results. Sometimes the best return on the investment you make in a relationship doesn't find you for years (or even *decades*) after the foundational work is complete.

3. Expect nothing in return.

I've already made this point in the title to this chapter, but it's worth repeating. If you keep your expectations low, you'll never be disappointed if things don't shake out to the good.

4. Ask smarter, not harder.

When you get to that place where you've established the kind of goodwill that allows you to make a re-quest or ask a favor, make sure your ask is specific, time-sensitive, and appropriate in the context of the relationship. A lot of times, we waste our relationship capital by asking for inconsequential favors, or we make requests that are vague, elusive, or unrealistic. Don't ask for something the other person is not in a position to deliver.

5. Manage expectations.

Yours . . . *and* the other person's. Know what you hope to get out of the relationship, know what you're prepared to give, and know how you'll find a way to meet in the middle so that both parties are served.

POWER FACT Recognition counts—way more than you might think. And in some cases it counts more than tangible rewards—like a bigger paycheck. That's what we learn from a survey of over 1,200 workers conducted by the employee motivation firm Make Their Day: Over 70 percent of them reported that the most meaningful form of recognition they'd received in the workplace had no dollar value, and 83 percent said recognition for contributions was more fulfilling than any rewards and gifts.

Chapter 13

BANK YOUR RELATIONSHIP CAPITAL

" I love it when a plan comes together."

If you grew up on '80s television like I did, you'll recognize that line from *The A-Team*. Back in the day, it was one of those television catchphrases that spilled into the culture. You'd see it on T-shirts and bumper stickers, but you'd mostly hear it whenever a bunch of moving parts lined up in just the right way to make it seem like whatever had magically or accidentally happened had been the plan all along.

Yep, I love it when a plan comes together, and you can make the case that the last of these elements we'll take a look at here is like the glue that holds all the rest together.

Without it, you'll never *really* be in a position to grab at the power in the room in a way that brings you any closer to your goals.

I'm talking here about the care and feeding of our *relationship capital*—an essential asset in every successful individual's personal and professional tool kit, and the key to unlocking your *powershift* potential.

In corporations, relationship capital usually refers both to all relationships within an organization *and* to those external relationships that help to drive business forward. It's the human bond that we develop with colleagues, with vendors, and among any combination of individuals or groups of individuals who have come to rely on one another to get a job done. But as individuals, and as small business owners and entrepreneurs, our relationship capital can be our single greatest asset.

Think of your relationship capital in this way:

- It's the network of friends and associates you've developed over the years, who may or may not be in a position to give you a boost or cut you a break or move your mission forward.

- It's the reserve of goodwill you've built up on the back of your good name and your extra efforts.

- It's the sum total of every time a colleague or even a competitor has turned to you with gratitude and said, "I owe you one."

With me, it just worked out that I've been able to build a hefty relationship bankroll over the years. How? By being true to myself and the way I was raised. By being consistent, persistent, straightforward. By always trying to treat people fairly, to carry myself with dignity and purpose, to work tirelessly in pursuit of my goals. All of that good stuff adds up, but it's not like I set out and made a calculated effort in this area. I was just out there doing my thing, daily, and it left me in a strong position to call on pretty much anyone I ever had any dealings with, anyone I ever partnered with or worked with on a project, reaching all the way back to high school.

For example, when things were firing on all cylinders at FUBU, and we were working late into the night in our offices on the sixty-sixth floor of the Empire State Building, I always made it a special point to have a kind word or make some show of appreciation to the security guard working the night shift by the elevator bank downstairs, or the cleaning crew that came in to empty our wastebaskets and straighten things up. Always, I wanted these good people to know that I valued their time and their work—not because I was trying to butter them up, but because my mother always taught me to respect hard work, no matter what that work was, who was doing it, or how much money they were making.

I'm all about the personal touches when it comes to maintaining relationships. When I give one of my keynote addresses, or when I sit down to consult with a company, for example, I make it a point to follow up with a handwritten note thanking my hosts for inviting me in to talk to this or that group. I don't do this with any thought to getting invited back, because nine times out of ten, when someone brings you in to deliver a speech, they're not looking to bring you back the next year. Nobody wants to hear from the same keynote speaker, year after year. They're out to mix things up, right? I do this because I always want to be adding to my list of friends and contacts. In the Rolodex I keep in my head, I can never run out of room, because you never know when you might need to call on someone for an assist or a solid. Plus, if someone does me a good turn, I want to let them know that I'm available to them on the bounce. It's the right thing to do—even when there's nothing in it for you.

Here's the one thing it helps to remember as you set off looking to develop a support network of friends and colleagues: **Treat people fairly and they'll remember you.** That's been the story of my life and career, and it can be your story, too. Keep in mind, however, that **just because people remember you in a positive way doesn't necessarily mean they will drop whatever they're doing to help you out in a tough spot.** Sometimes they will, sometimes they won't . . . depends on the time you've put into that relationship, and how recently you've put in that time. Depends on what else is going on with them when you make the ask. Depends on a lot of other variables, actually, but the constant in this scenario is that our relationships matter.

Every relationship matters.

Every piece makes up the whole just like in the fashion

business, where if you cut even the smallest swatch from a garment you're left with a funny-looking garment. Whatever your business, whatever your situation, if you cut even a few relationships out of your life—or behave in such a way that others cut *you* from their lives—well, then the pieces won't fit together in the best possible way.

A couple things to keep in mind:

- Try to remember how hungry you were two years ago, five years ago, ten years ago, whatever the case may be, and find a way to attach it to the hunger of the person you're dealing with across the table.

- Whatever you're doing, do more—meaning, if you've gotten in the habit of arriving at your desk at a certain time, try to get there a little earlier, or stay later . . . or maybe spend a little extra time honing your pitch or making sure your sales presentation really pops.

- Go out of your way to extend a kindness—to your employees, to your co-workers, to your customers . . . get in the habit of sending handwritten notes or personal cards—in our digital age, these kinds of special touches really stand out.

- If you've gotten in the habit of going to your annual trade show a day or two late, or leaving a day or two early, get out of that habit immediately—you'll never know who might be pinching your customer base or making inroads onto your turf on those days you've been missing.

- And finally, if you catch yourself using a line like "I'll have my people call your people," go ahead and kick yourself, hard—a line like that, it's a sure sign you're losing touch, because you just can't delegate a personal relationship.

Now, I know there are people out there who make it a special point to take the same care in treating people right, but they don't always get the same love or respect on the rebound because whatever it is they're putting out doesn't necessarily come from an authentic place. So I guess what I'm saying here is that you need to actually *be* a good person if you hope to bring other good people onboard. **You can't just play at being kind or decent or grateful— people will see right through you!** So over this next bunch of pages I'm just going to go ahead and assume you're all the real deal.

RESPECT THE OTHER PERSON'S TIME

One of the best ways to illustrate the importance of taking care of your relationship capital is to look at how protective people can be about their social networks. Now, I understand a lot of people go on social media literally just for fun, but be mindful of how other people view your consumption. We all know on some level that it's possible to build our relationships in this way, but how do we begin to tap the power they hold?

Well, if you've been able to develop a sizable following on social media, you already have a good idea. When people decide to follow you or to pay any kind of attention to what you're putting out online, it's like you've entered into a social contract. They will stay with you as long as you don't post with your chest out or abuse your platform by spewing anger or hate, or by pretending to be someone or something other than who or what you are. You're careful not to waste your followers' time with frivolous posts, and on the other side of the bargain your followers are respectful of your time and interests as well. At some point, you even start to pay attention to what you're "liking" or commenting on, because you don't want to fill up other people's feeds with stuff that might be important only to you. And get this: If your social media footprint puts you at some kind of "influencer" level and you're being compensated for highlighting a product or an establishment in a positive way, then chances are you're particularly aware of what an endorsement from you can mean online, and so you'll start to be more and more thoughtful about who or what you support . . . and *why*.

Lindsey Vonn happens to be very active on social media—and she's damn good at it. One of the things she's damn good at is being *very* particular about the brands or products she endorses to her nearly two million Instagram followers. She'll shout out to one of her own fashion or health and nutrition businesses, but if she decides to give a boost to someone else's business you can bet it has been vetted and considered and reconsidered before she puts it into play. Lindsey knows those two million people didn't sign on to her platform to be hustled or sold to. They're fans, mostly, and they want to follow Lindsey's comings and goings, learn about her workout routines, maybe share in her adventures, or be inspired by her fashion choices. In fact, she's so careful not to take advantage of her supporters in this way, she's started separate social media accounts to promote the good work she does with her foundation, which is dedicated to empowering young girls, and with her individual businesses. She even has an Instagram account for her dogs!

The same kind of thinking applies to the people in your *actual* network. You don't want to be anything less than transparent with those relationships, and you certainly don't want to abuse them in any way. You want to honor whatever it was that brought you together in the first place, which of course is what can keep you together going forward. You don't want those relationships to start to feel like they're all about you. These people are on your side because they felt a certain connection at one time or another and wanted to align themselves with you in some way. So you need to bring the same care and attention to those relationships that you would bring to a Facebook friend with a habit of posting pictures of her cat.

Look, it's tempting to use the relationships you've built as collateral to generate new, more impactful relationships or opportunities. I *get* that, but that's the quickest way to bank-rupt your entire network. While it's certainly appropriate to share connections with others, you want to make sure there's buy-in from both parties before making introductions. And before you even reach out to bring two parties together, make sure there's real potential for gain for all involved.

Exploiting, overleveraging, or otherwise taxing your network is a mistake that's hard to reverse, so here I want to encourage you to start thinking of your re-lationship capital as a kind of currency: You only have so much to go around, and it can only take you so far. Treat it the way you would the money in your bank account. On the one hand, you should always be looking for ways to deposit new relationships into that account before drawing down on the ones already in place, but at the same time you should be working to strengthen and grow the rela-tionships you already have in savings.

With an *actual* bank account or investment portfolio, people are always looking to raise the bottom line. We like to watch our assets grow, right? We work like crazy to be able to live off our income instead of our savings, and we're reluctant to spend down our capital unless it's for an essential expenditure like a new car or a down payment on a house.

But when you're looking to make a meaningful *powershift,*

it's actually not that different from making a big life-changing purchase like buying a home. You're going to have to put some of the assets you've spent a lifetime building into play.

LET THE WORLD KNOW YOU'RE GOING PLACES

One of the great blessings of my life these days is the chance to work with young visionaries and hard chargers who carry the same "rise and grind" and "power of broke" mindset as I did when I was just starting out. They're powering into their futures—and just like we were in the early days of FUBU, a lot of them are figuring it out on the fly. But for every seat-of-the-pants, make-it-up-as-I-go-along entrepreneur I meet who reminds me of myself as a young man, there's a super-savvy, super-dedicated innovator or game-changer going about their business in an organized, carefully orchestrated way.

"Steph Korey, the cofounder of Away, one of the hottest luggage brands, falls in that second category. As I'm finishing up writing this book, some stories have come to light about negative aspects of Away's culture, and Steph has admitted that she's working on improving her management and leadership skills. But here I want to focus on how this young woman and her cofounder embodied the *powershift* principles in the way they built Away from the ground up. There's no debating that Steph and her partner, Jen Rubio, have shaken up their industry, and you'll see their passion is clearly contagious."

Get Steph Korey talking about luggage and travel, and you can see it's like a mission for her . . . a calling. "Our hope with Away is to inspire people to live a life of new experiences," Steph explains—and, gotta say, she lives the truth of that statement.

One of the ways she originally put her passion into play was by drawing down on the relationship capital she was able to build by working at two successful start-ups *before* pivoting into the luggage business. After graduating from Brown University, she got a job at the pioneering online eyewear company Warby Parker. Then, while getting her MBA at Columbia University in Manhattan, she signed on to work at Casper, the pioneering online mattress company.

You'll note here that I described each of those start-ups as *pioneering*. That's the rep that sticks to a successful e-commerce business that's first to act in a market segment. It's also the rep that sticks to people who were in on the ground floor of that business. Doesn't matter if they were the CEO or the person who ran the market research . . . there's winning street cred that becomes a part of their personal history, just by association. That's why, when Steph and her partner started reaching out to investors, there was a certain pedigree to their pitch—meaning, Steph was able to trade on her résumé to help open doors and give investors confidence that she and her partner had what it would take to get their idea off the ground.

But it's what she *did* once she got inside those doors tha really made a difference in Away's early fundraising efforts: She set it up so that she wasn't looking for something from potential investors, but offering them an opportunity. And one of the reasons that opportunity might have appeared so attractive to some was because Steph had played a role in these other successful launches.

"The fact that Jen and I both had previous experience at high-growth e-commerce start-ups definitely gave us an added layer of credibility," she says. "That background gave potential investors greater confidence that we had what it took as a duo to get our idea off the ground."

STEPH KOREY, on her pitch to investors: "From the beginning, Jen and I felt a lot of conviction about our vision and that we'd be inviting potential investors to be a part of something special. I think approaching investor meetings with that frame of mind that we weren't asking for charity, but instead offering investors an opportunity, helped to us to feel more confident in our ask. We made sure to always lead with our vision for Away that went beyond just luggage. We've always envisioned Away to be broadly about travel and how we can transform the market altogether."

The idea for Away gets me thinking back to the *item–label–brand–lifestyle* progression I wrote about earlier, because, like I said, most people don't spend a whole lot of time thinking about luggage. Oh, there are name-brand manufacturers like Samsonite and American Tourister, but there isn't a whole lot of brand loyalty. I know in my own experience I've had a bunch of bags over the years that I bought on an impulse, and they maybe lasted for a couple trips before they wound up in the back of the closet or lost a wheel or whatever.

Steph and her partner had it in their heads that road warriors like myself wanted what they called a "more seamless" travel experience, but before they set to work on a prototype they backed up their ideas with extensive market research. They wanted to understand how people packed, what they thought about the suitcases they already had, what they'd like to see in the *next* suitcase they might buy. They called on hundreds of family members, friends, and friends-of-friends to help them *focus-group* and troubleshoot their design concepts. Granted, these were people inclined to participate and help out however they could, but only because Steph and Jen had established a certain reputation. Even among their friends and family, it was known that these two women were the real deal, off in serious pursuit of an exciting, viable opportunity, and their friends and family trusted that their input would be valued. If these people were ever made to feel that their time was being wasted, or that they weren't contributing in a meaningful way, they would have been out the door in the time it took to say "See you at Thanksgiving."

Out of that data, Steph and Jen began to design what they believed to be the ultimate carry-on—with two compartments, a battery able to hold up to five full charges for your phone or laptop, a lightweight shell, and wheels that spin all the way around.

Customers went crazy for that carry-on. Steph knows,

because she asked. Again and again. She was determined to give her early customers and potential customers a voice—to build up that relationship capital *before* the company was up and running. Early on, Steph and her partner relied heavily on word of mouth and on a first-of-its-kind social media platform that encouraged people to share their travel adventures. It was Jen who ran the social media side of things, but between the two of them they made sure that every customer who interacted with the company had a positive, ongoing experience.

"We took care to nurture each of those relationships," Steph tells me, "making sure specific feedback was included in the conversation every step of the way."

I'm reminded here of something my friend Jay Abraham always says about the three ways you can deal with a customer. Jay's probably one of the smartest people I know in the area of direct response marketing, so when he talks about how to grow or nourish your customer base I'm all over it. According to Jay, you can acquire a new customer, up-sell a current customer, or create an incentive for an existing customer to buy more frequently. Here, I think Steph and Jen found a way to do Jay one better by putting a fourth element into play—they found a way to get a dialogue going with their customers, to help create a sense of buy-in, and to tinker with their product so that they were better able to keep their customers satisfied.

In this way, and in so many others, Steph was determined to bank tons of relationship capital, knowing that at some point she'd have to start drawing it down. Every customer they engaged was like a deposit in the bank, and soon those customers were made to feel like they were part of a community and all that it stood for: superior, smart, stylish luggage for the superior, smart, stylish traveler. Very quickly, Away achieved *lifestyle* status and now offers a full range of travel products, including backpacks and luggage tags.

Investors have taken note. Away's valuation as of their last round of financing was an astonishing $1.4 billion. That's right—$1.4 billion. (Here, let me throw in an exclamation point!) That's a number Steph could have never even imagined when she and Jen set off on this journey, but to hear her tell it, that feeling didn't come close to the thrill she experienced the first time she saw a traveler board a plane out of JFK carrying one of her suitcases—the first time it wasn't being carried by a friend or family member, that is.

"Since then, each time we launch a new product or hit a new milestone, we're overwhelmed by the response from our community," she says. "So the feeling has never really gone away."

SPEND YOUR CAPITAL WISELY

Steph's story has got me thinking of all the different ways we can tap our relationship capital for our *personal* brands as well.

Some things to keep in mind as you look to grow your game in this way:

1. Grow your network deeper, not wider.

Most people equate the size of their social network with its potential impact, but even a small network can produce big results. What counts is the quality of your relationships, not the quantity. Do you go out of your way to make people feel a part of your community? Are you able to show your appreciation in an organic, ongoing way? Is there a true feeling of engagement? Obviously, you want to expand your reach and your network, but before you get ahead of yourself why not look at the connections you already have and see if you can maybe find a way to strengthen them? One thing I've been doing lately is identifying three to five relationships each week that I'd like to build upon. What I'll do is reach out to that person, or that community, for no specific reason other than to check in, and out of that we're usually able to get a dialogue going that may lead to an entirely new initiative.

2. Systemize your outreach.

It might seem strange to build systems around relationship management, but there are simple tools you can use to track your network's growth that can pay huge dividends for you or your company.

3. Tap into the power of relationship R&D.

There's a ton of information out there that can be enormously useful as you build your network and look to make a lasting impression. Whenever I'm about to meet with someone face-to-face, I'll spend a couple minutes online checking that person out—not in a *stalk-y* kind of way, but in a *research-y* kind of way. Take the time to learn about that person's latest projects, their current interests or whereabouts, and you'll gather bits and pieces of personal information that will help to boost rapport and fast-track a stronger connection.

4. Protect and preserve your network.

This goes back to a point I made earlier about being careful with the way you "spend down" your relationship capital. Think long and hard before reaching out to one of your contacts with a meaningful ask, or before putting two individuals or groups together on an initiative. There are only so many plays to be made, so you don't want to burn through all of them right out of the gate.

5. Know the terms of your relationship.

I don't know about you, but I interact differently with different people ... for different reasons. So before reaching out to someone, it pays to know how that person likes to receive information. When I'm looking to get in touch with Mark Cuban, for example, I know he's not a phone guy. I am. But if I want something from Mark, I'll need to play his game. People who know me know I'm not a long-email person and that it's better to pick up the phone and call than it is to send me a long-winded email I'll never get around to reading. My friend Gary Vaynerchuck likes to move about the planet, so even though we both live in New York City we've met for dinner in faraway places like Mexico, because that's when he has the time to sit down and chill. The idea is to hit people up in ways that fit with their habits and lifestyle—and in the moment, to bend yours to suit. Let them play *your* game when they want something from *you*.

POWER FACT It's not just what you know but who you know. According to a LinkedIn survey I saw recently that 70 percent of those interviewed landed their current jobs because they knew someone at the company. So dust off your LinkedIn profile, and keep up with your contacts, because when you're looking to make a *powershift* and seize a new opportunity, you want to be sure to give yourself every advantage.

IN CONCLUSION . . .

Okay, so we've talked about ways you can build influence and make the right kind of noise to get people to lean your way. We've spent some time on making deals happen and negotiating from a position of strength. And we've looked at the importance of cultivating strong relationships and making a shared history with our contacts and colleagues. Now the thing to do is put all three of these elements on blast and get them to work for you as you *powershift* into your future.

Chapter 14

THE *POWERSHIFT* PLAY

Throughout this book, I've focused on the three different skill sets we need to master if we hope to bring about powerful change.

Here they are again, for reinforcement:

- You've got to establish your cred, build influence . . . **make an impression.**

- You've got to build up your negotiation chops and bargain from a place of strength . . . **make a deal.**

- You've got to build relationships, feed them over time, and put together acres and acres of common ground with people who will become more and more inclined to lean your way or cut you some slack ... **make relationships last.**

Got that? That's great, but what you also need to get is that the *power* in my *powershift* principle comes from all these moving parts working together. This needs reinforcing, too. We're not just out to tick off these boxes, one by one, and move on to the next set of skills. We need to think of it more like a game of three-level chess. Sure, you can put your focus into winning at one level, and that will always serve you in the short run or in a very specific way. But if you're out to put yourself in a position to make a sudden, meaningful, unexpected move in a whole new direction ... not just once, but over time ... well then, you've got to put in the hard work of getting people to root for you and believe in you *and* the hard work of negotiating the right deals for you and your partners *and* honoring the many relationships you've collected over the years.

Again: You need to focus on your past, your present, *and* your future ... all at once.

Like I said at the outset, I was blessed early on in my career to have all of these pieces working in sync without really having to think about them. I just did my thing and there they were. But after a while, *doing my thing* didn't come to me so easily. Or even when it did, I couldn't explain it in such a way that I might find a way to grow my game—or even to just repeat the winning steps I might have stumbled onto in the first place. I had to look back at all the moves I'd made as a young man and find a way to replicate them as I got older and stepped into a totally new arena.

Basically, I went looking for a template I could follow—one I could share with readers out to move the needle in their own lives and careers.

DO THE RIGHT THING

I've got a story to close things out that shows all these elements at play.

Early on in our FUBU run, there was a *People* magazine article that sent a little light our way. We'd gotten a bunch of local press to this point, but this was our first national article. They called me "a CEO to watch," which I thought was kind of cool, but it was mostly kind of cool that they'd said our products were hot. It was enough just to be featured, you know—a real *pinch me* kind of moment.

One day during that week when this particular issue was on the stands, I got a letter from Spike Lee. Yeah, *that* Spike Lee. It was just sitting there in my pile of mail on my desk, and it had the name of his production company as the return address, so I was excited as hell as I tore it open.

You have to realize, Spike Lee meant a whole lot to our community back then—still does, but this was a game-changing time in African American culture. It was about ten years after Spike blew up with *She's Gotta Have It* and *Do the Right Thing,* so he was already an established icon, especially in and around New York City. This letter showed up right around the time he was doing those crazy Nike commercials featuring Michael Jordan and Spike's Mars Blackmon character, the kid who was obsessed with his Air Jordans, so his influence was everywhere. On top of all that, Spike had his own Forty Acres and a Mule clothing line going—so in some ways we were competitors, I guess.

I had no idea why Spike was reaching out, wasn't even sure the letter was from Spike himself. I mean, it could have been from someone in his company—an assistant, maybe, or a lawyer hitting me up with some kind of "cease and desist" letter claiming we'd knocked off one of his designs. Could have been anything. But sure enough, the letter was from Spike, short and sweet, congratulating me on the *People* article.

Let me tell you . . . that letter was something. It was special. Meant the world. Just the *idea* of it, you know. But it was the way Spike signed it that really struck me and stayed with me over the years.

He wrote, "I see you."

That's all. Just those three little words. *I see you.* And in those three little words there was enormous power. There was validation. There was solidarity. And I held on to all of that as I charged into my future.

Like I said, it was special. And when you place it in context, it was even more special, because this was at a time when there was this idea out there that to make it in business you had to run everybody over on your way to the top. Probably that started to take shape when the movie *Wall Street* came out, which put it out there that greed was good, and that all was fair in the name of a dollar. Even within the African American community there was this sense that it was every man for himself, eat or be eaten—that was the mentality. I didn't buy in to any of that, but it was out there, so for me to get this letter from Spike, out of the blue, it was powerful. Validating. Real.

I see you.

I cherished that letter, and carried it with me—not *literally,* of course. I tucked it away to keep it safe, but I carried it with me in my heart, and more than twenty years later, when Spike finally received an Academy Award for the screenplay for *BlacKkKlansman,* I thought about it immediately.

The night he won the Oscar, I'd managed to score an invite to the *Vanity Fair* after-party, which people kept telling me was one of the hardest parties to get into. I never believed them, because they always seemed to invite me, so their standards couldn't be too, too high. (Just sayin'!) I was already there when Spike came in, and as you can imagine, the place went nuts. It's like this sea of people parted to make way for Spike as he crossed the room with his Oscar—it was a cool thing to see, a real hero's welcome.

Now, I'd run into Spike a few times over the years, but I'd never brought up that letter or told him what it meant to me. I was too intimidated by him. He was playing at a whole other level. But that all changed the night Spike got his Oscar. Not because I was suddenly playing at his level—no way. I was still nowhere close to being his peer, nowhere near his equal. But what changed was that I had

been moving about the planet with a whole lot more confidence, following this career evolution that found me with
Shark Tank. I'd *powershifted* onto this entirely new platform,
was looking out at the world with a fresh set of eyes . . . whatever.

I left Spike alone for the next little while to work the
room and collect the backslaps and bro-hugs he had coming, but I caught up to him eventually. And when I did, I
congratulated him and said, "I see you."

That's all.

He remembered the letter, of course. But I think it surprised him, a little bit, that *I* had remembered the letter. I
mean, it had been more than twenty years! But I brought it
up that night for the way it seemed to bring us full circle.
Not me and Spike, because it's not like we were pals or had
been through any kind of wringer together. No, the full-
circle piece, for me, was the way those words seemed to
connect the young men we were back in the day to the
somewhat older men we had become. We'd set out to make
a mark, each of us in our own way. We'd been able to make
some kind of difference, each of us in our own way. And
just as Spike had once thought to let me know that someone else was watching me, appreciating me, looking out for
me, I wanted him to know that people were watching him,
appreciating him, looking out for him.

Even though we didn't know each other all that well,
Spike and I had shared a twenty-year history that had this
powershift concept written all over it. But neither one of us
was trading on any of that power that night of the Oscars—

this wasn't about *that*. This was about me finding a way to honor and deepen a relationship that had meant a lot to me as I was coming up, a relationship I hoped would continue to mean a lot to me in the future. And on Spike's side of the deal, on the receiving end of this exchange, there was the power that came in knowing that his words and his influence had made a real impact on the life of a young man out to speak into the culture and continue the conversation Spike himself had helped to start.

Transform any situation . . .

Close any deal . . .

Achieve any outcome . . .

That's the promise of this book—says so right there in the subtitle. And in this one simple exchange, played out over twenty years, I saw the *powershift* principle on full display. So if you take away just one thing from this book, I hope it's this: When you play the game to win on all three levels, you truly can achieve just about anything.

I see you.

And I hope I've inspired you to get out there and shift your power in any direction you want to go.

SHOW A LITTLE LOVE

Before signing off, I want to give a final shout-out to the dozen or so influencers, change agents, and *powershifters* who agreed to share their experiences and insights for this book. I've found in my previous books that readers really respond to real-world examples of some of the ideas and strategies under discussion, and I'm honored to be able to add their stories to the conversation.

If, like me, you've been inspired by their stories and the many creative, resilient, relentless ways they've succeeded in shifting power back to their side of the table in their lives and careers, I hope you'll join me in continuing to follow them on social media as they continue to make an impression, make empowering deals, and build the kinds of lasting relationships that bring about meaningful change.

You can find them here:

- **MARK CUBAN**—follow my *Shark Tank* partner on Instagram: @mcuban . . . on Twitter: @mcuban . . . follow the Dallas Mavericks on Instagram: @dallasmavs . . . on Twitter: @dallasmavs

- **BETHENNY FRANKEL**—follow the former *Real Housewives* star and Skinnygirl founder on Instagram: @bethennyfrankel . . . on Twitter: @Bethenny . . . brand: @skinnygirl

- **RANDY GOLDBERG AND DAVID HEATH**—follow the founders of Bombas, "the most comfortable socks in the history of feet," on Instagram: @BOMBAS . . . on Twitter: @BOMBAS

- **KRIS JENNER**—follow one of the world's most forward-thinking influencers on Instagram: @krisjenner . . . on Twitter: @KrisJenner . . . follow *Keeping Up with the Kardashians* on Instagram: @KUWTK . . . on Twitter: @KUWTK

- **BILLIE JEAN KING**—follow a true pioneer in women's sports on Instagram: @billiejeanking . . . on Twitter: @BillieJeanKing

- **STEPH KOREY**—follow the serial entrepreneur and change agent on Instagram: @stephkorey . . . on Twitter: @stephkorey . . . follow Away on Instagram: @Away . . . on Twitter: @away

- **CLAY NEWBILL**—follow the *Shark Tank* executive producer on Instagram: @cnewbill1 . . . on Twitter: @ClayNewbill . . . follow *Shark Tank* on Instagram: @sharktankabc . . . on Twitter: @ABCSharkTank

- **PITBULL**—follow the Miami-born rapper and global music superstar on Instagram: @pitbull . . . on Twitter: @pitbull

- **CHARLYNDA SCALES**—follow the founder of Mutt's Sauce on Instagram: @charlyndajean . . . on Twitter: @MsVetAmerica2RU . . . follow Mutt's Sauce on Instagram: @muttssauce . . . on Twitter: @MuttsSauce

- **BILLY GENE SHAW**—follow the game-changing online marketer on Instagram: @billygeneismarketing . . . on Twitter: @askbillygene

- **CRYSTAL VOLINCHAK**—follow The Shark Group's virtual assistant on Instagram: @crystalvolinchak

- **LINDSEY VONN**—follow one of the greatest skiers of all time on Instagram: @lindseyvonn . . . on Twitter: @lindseyvonn . . . (for an extra dash of cuteness, follow Lindsey's dogs on Instagram: @ su_vonndogs)

Oh, and speaking of cuteness, and since we opened the book with a story about the most influential *powershifter* I know, you might want to follow my daughter Minka as well:

- **MINKA JOHN**—on Instagram: @minkajaggerjohn

As always, you can let me know your thoughts about this book, share your *powershift* stories with me and your fellow readers, and tell what kind of ground you'd like to see me cover in my next book. I'd love to hear from you . . .

- **DAYMOND JOHN**—on Instagram: @theshark daymond . . . on Twitter: @thesharkdaymond

ACKNOWLEDGMENTS

There are so many people that I'm grateful for every single day. My family, my friends, my partners, my co-workers, my supporters—thank you all for pushing me to continue to grow and strive to reach my goals. You all know who you are, and I could not have created *Powershift* or embodied these strategies and principles throughout my life without your unwavering support. And I of course have to thank you, the reader. If it wasn't for your continuous dedication and loyalty, I would not be able to use my platform to reach such a wide audience. It is because of you that I can continue to share my knowledge and experiences and help others achieve their goals and find success.

INDEX

About the Author

DAYMOND JOHN is the founder and CEO of FUBU, a celebrated global lifestyle brand with more than $6 billion in sales that he built from the ground up. He is among the country's most visible entrepreneurs as one of the stars of ABC's Emmy Award–winning series *Shark Tank*. Daymond is also the author of the *New York Times* instant best-selling books *Rise and Grind* and *The Power of Broke*. He has received more than thirty-five esteemed awards, including Brandweek Marketer of the Year, Ernst & Young's Master Entrepreneur of the Year, NAACP Image Award for Outstanding Literary Work, and the Essence Award, and he was appointed a Presidential Ambassador for Global Entrepreneurship under President Obama. Daymond is also the CEO of The Shark Group, a premier New York City–based consulting firm whose clients range from Fortune 500 companies to new media businesses to celebrities. His rags-to-riches inspirational background and his unwavering determination to succeed couple for a motivational lesson, and his skill in the way he expresses this story to others has earned him recognition as a top speaker in the country. Daymond has proven himself to be an icon within the fashion world and a strategic and savvy businessman who can recognize what companies to invest in or establish partnerships with. These partnerships with companies like Chase for Business, AARP, Shopify, and many others reflect Daymond's esteemed reputation.

About the Type

This book was set in Bembo, a typeface based on an old-style Roman face that was used for Cardinal) Pietro Bembo's tract *De Aetna* in 1495. Bembo was cut by Francesco Griffo (1450–1518) in the early sixteenth century for Italian Renaissance printer and publisher Aldus Manutius (1449–1515). The Lanston Monotype Company of Philadelphia brought the well-proportioned letterforms of Bembo to the United States in the 1930s.

Also from *New York Times* bestselling author

DAYMOND JOHN

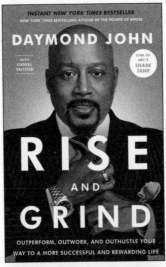

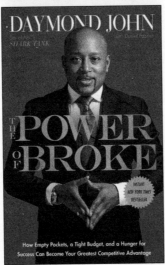